Papers presented to Section F (Economics)
at the 1975 Annual Meeting of the
British Association for the Advancement of Science

Economics and Equality

Edited by Rt Hon. Aubrey Jones

Philip Allan

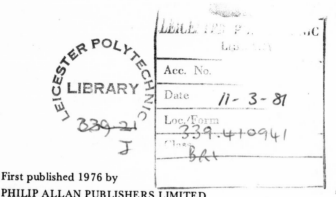
First published 1976 by

PHILIP ALLAN PUBLISHERS LIMITED
RED LION COTTAGE
MARKET PLACE
DEDDINGTON
OXFORD OX5 4SE

© Philip Allan Publishers 1976

0 86003 010 5 (hardback)
0 86003 111 X (paperback)

Printed in Great Britain by The Camelot Press Limited, Southampton.

Contents

Introduction

Much of Victorian fiction appears to have been concerned with the 'condition of England', by which expression is meant, not the historical status of the country, but the manner of living of the poorer among its people. The Industrial Revolution undoubtedly enhanced the material prosperity of Britain; this enhanced prosperity must, even if in only small degree, have percolated downwards to the least of its inhabitants; but the overwhelming impression left by the novels is one of deepened oppression.

> Surely no one could now consider Mrs. Gaskell's books — interesting though they are as documents of their period — to be reliable sources of information about the lives of the working people, still less about their thoughts or their political activities. Still less are the works of Kingsley and Disraeli in intention or effect sources to be taken with any but the most careful counter-checking. Yet these are the voices heard most often . . .

The above paragraph summarises the lecture given by Mr Michael Jefferson to Section F of the British Association in August 1975. And he undoubtedly has something. I have heard of an American author — whom I have not read — who, from a study of children's books, claims to be able to foretell the state of the relevant country a generation later. Perhaps the novels of one generation affect the children's books of a second, which in turn determine the political preoccupations of a third. Certainly for the greater part of my political lifetime the thoughts of politicians have been predominantly concerned not with Britain in the world, but with the 'condition of England'. It is fitting therefore that Section F should choose this for its theme for 1975, subtly renaming it by a more modern expression — 'Equality'.

The expression 'equality' is more modern because the older expression 'condition of England' was synonymous with poverty, and poverty, while not eliminated, has, thanks to a great deal of social service legislation, been considerably diminished. 'Equality' is more up-to-date, too, because, as Professor Harbury points out, we live in an age of mass consumption in which the more luxurious ways we might covet are nightly displayed before us on television; it is also an age in which governments of different colours endeavour to secure a stable economy through such things as incomes policies, and how can they hope to win acceptance for such innovations without regard to 'equality'?

Now there are two kinds of inequality: in income and in wealth; and of these the greater is that in wealth. According to Dr. Harrison two thirds of the personal wealth of the country are owned by one tenth of the population. Not that there have been lacking attempts by governments to redress both kinds of inequality — that in income through taxes rising progressively the higher the income, and that in capital through a tax on an estate passing to somebody else on the death of the owner. But, according to the speakers appearing before Section F, governmental efforts have not had all that effect. As far as income is concerned, there would appear to have been a transfer from those well off to those somewhat less well off, 'while the lower half of the distribution has done no more than roughly maintain its share of the total'. And, as far as capital goes, to quote Dr. Harrison, '. . . although the share of the top 1% has fallen quite substantially, groups just below the top 1% have increased their share of personal wealth so that, at least since 1936, most of the redistribution which has occurred has been within the top 20%'.

Not unnaturally, speakers called for a change in the taxation system. Professor Harbury was 'for switching from income to wealth and wealth transfer taxation'. Professor Sandford was equally in favour of wealth transfer taxes, including a heavier capital gains tax, and explicitly supported an accessions tax, i.e. 'a tax levied on the beneficiary of a legacy or gift, the tax on any one receipt being determined by the total amount received by way of legacies and gifts'. I might modestly add that, more years ago than I care to remember, I suggested a not dissimilar tax in a House of Commons debate on the Finance Bill; I innocently imagined that the Chancellor of the Exchequer was more receptive to new ideas than he turned out to be.

I have so far mentioned those speakers at the session who clearly felt that the present distribution of income and wealth was unjust and plainly wanted to do something about it. It so happens that they were all economists. But what, it may be asked, has it to do with economists, *qua* economists, whether the distribution of income and wealth is just or unjust (whatever those last two adjectives may mean)? Why should economists express a 'value judgement' (pejorative expression, that!) of this kind? Is not this a matter for politicians? And is not economics a 'pure' science, possibly telling politicians how to achieve given goals but not setting the goals for them?

There are two interesting papers on this topic: that by Professor Hutchison entitled 'Economists and Social Justice in the History of Economic Thought', and that by Mr Tutton on 'Intellectual Conceptions of Economic Justice'. In the days of Adam Smith, or rather according to the picture presented in *The Wealth of Nations*, participants in markets were small; each, pursuing his own end, was guided by a blind hand which led him to act in a manner beneficient to all; and what was coincided with what ought to be. There was no need therefore to be concerned with the distribution of wealth. The point was brutally put by Senior:

> The questions: to what extent and under what circumstances the possession of wealth is, on the whole, beneficial or injurious to its possessor, or to the society of which he is a member? what distribution of wealth is most desirable in each different state of society? and what are the means by which any given country can facilitate such a distribution? — all these are questions of great interest and difficulty, but no more form part of the Science of Political Economy, in which we use the term, than navigation forms part of the Science of Astronomy.

Despite this statement of objective neutrality by Senior, Ricardo had no doubts as to what he thought was the 'right' distribution of wealth:

> . . . the quantity of employment in the country must depend, not only on the quantity of capital, but upon its advantageous distribution, and, above all, on the conviction of each capitalist that he will be allowed to enjoy un- molested the fruits of his capital, his skill, and his enterprise. To take from him this conviction is at once to annihilate half the productive industry of the country, and would be more fatal to the poor labourer than to the rich capitalist himself. This is so self-evident, that men very little advanced beyond the very lowest stations in the country cannot be ignorant of it, and it may be doubted whether any large number even of the lowest would, if they could, promote a division of property.

A fundamental change occurred in the later decades of the century. There were two causes. The first was the advent of Marshall who had been drawn into the study of economics by an interest in practical ethics and who devoted himself to the problem of poverty, 'and very little of my work has been devoted to any inquiry which does not bear upon that'. The second cause was the attempt on the part of economists once again to have it both ways — that is, to prescribe policies for politicians while maintaining the 'purity' or the objective neutrality of economics. For example, Edgeworth adduced the principle of utility or personal satisfaction to justify progressive taxation. Since the utility of a given product must be greater for a poor man than for a rich man, the social welfare would be greater if the rich man were taxed and income redistributed to the poor man.

Pareto did not quite go so far, though he too attempted to enunciate a principle of optimum distribution also based on the concept of utility. He laid down the dictum that a given distribution could be said to have improved only when at least one person gained and no one else lost. Clearly this ruled out any redistributive taxation of the rich in favour of the poor. By the same token it excluded economists, *qua* pure economists, from an important field of policy-making. Pareto, however, brought them back in again with the problem of unemployment. Unemployment justified public works — which Ricardo would have anathematised — because they could be provided to the unemployed without taking away from the employed. From his grave, therefore, Pareto helped Keynes to overcome the ghost of Ricardo.

Marshall was possibly the first consciously to approach problems of economics via the route of ethics. In recent years he has been followed in this approach by Professor John Rawls of Harvard. Rawls explicitly rejects the utilitarian premise — the premise, that is, that each individual sets out to maximise his satisfaction, that the satisfactions of all individuals can be added up to a total, with the conclusion that that particular distribution of income and wealth is best which promotes the greatest satisfaction of the greatest number. Rawls comments, in my view rightly, that the idea of adding up the satisfactions of different people 'does not take seriously the distinction between persons'. Accordingly, he takes up a different starting-point. Suppose, he says, that individuals are in a state of nature but are about to form a society by entering into a social contract. No one will know anything of the potential of others, each will fear the worst for himself, with the

result that the distribution of income decided upon will differ
from that which emerges when a little is taken from Peter and
more is given to Paul so as to maximise the satisfaction of the
greatest number in a fully mature society.

This is clearly not the place to wade into the controversy
between utilitarianism and 'Rawlsism'. Suffice it to say that Mr
Paul Grout has sought to work out the implications of the two
philosophies for income tax, education and growth. Clearly, his
calculations are based on assumptions which have to be carefully
examined. Subject to that qualification his conclusions are
interesting. They are, first, that under the Rawlsian concept of
justice taxes on higher incomes would be higher than under
utilitarian principles, though lower than they today are in the
United Kingdom; secondly, that Rawlsian justice would lean
more towards a comprehensive system of education than to a
more selective one; and thirdly and finally, that the rate of
economic growth is likely to be lower under Rawlsian than under
utilitarian principles.

Clearly, economists have difficulty in maintaining both that
their science is 'pure' and that their intrusion into the field of
policy is based on unassailable ethical precepts. Perhaps Mr
Tutton is right in suggesting that economists are advocating
policies on solid ethical grounds only when the issues with which
they deal are blessed with a consensus. The trouble is that subjects move in and out of the consensus. That reasonably full
employment was desirable was once a matter of consensus; it has
now ceased to be. As Mr Tutton points out, Professor Meade, in
his latest book, *The Intelligent Radical's Guide to Economic
Policy,* does not even list the level of employment as one of the
'intelligent radical's' objectives of economic policy.

Perhaps the economists are, in political terms anyhow, premature in abandoning full employment as a desirable goal. A reading
of Mr George Woodcock's 'Trade Unions and Social Equality' and
of Mr Reisman's essay on the doctrines of Professor Galbraith
suggests that the problem of unemployment can be more usefully
seen in the context of institutions than in the context of 'pure'
economics. Perhaps indeed institutions have brought into being a
new 'trade-off' — the higher the level of employment, the more
difficult the introduction and the maintenance of an incomes
policy, and the higher the rate of inflation. Perhaps the trouble is
that economists have been too preoccupied with maintaining the
sanctity of their academic discipline and that their contributions

to policy-making would be more useful if combined with those from other disciplines. But to advance that thought too far would destroy the *raison d'etre* of Section F. And that is something which the writer of an introduction to Section F lectures ought not to do.

The Right Hon. Aubrey Jones
January 1976

RT HON. AUBREY JONES

1 The economics of equality

When I was first invited to give this lecture I realised I was likely
over the intervening months to be living and working abroad. I
was unlikely, therefore, to be able to keep up to date in my reading or to undertake such empirical work as I might think desirable.
If as a result in this talk I display ignorances I hope you will for-
give me.

The title of the talk — 'The Economics of Equality' — embodies
two conceivably contradictory notions which I suppose I am
expected to try and marry together. Theoretically, economics is
presumably concerned with the application of limited resources to
multiple ends; in other words, it is concerned with the efficiency
with which resources are used as determined by a certain standard.
In practice, economics can be concerned with the way in which in
fact incomes are determined or resources used, which need not
necessarily be the way in which theory suggests that they are determined or used. But either way, economics, whether theoretical or
descriptive, is ethically neutral; it incorporates no value judgement.
Equality, on the other hand, does incorporate a value judgement.
It has about it an ethical and a moral connotation, and because of
that connotation it has behind it considerable political force.

It would be difficult to exaggerate the strength of that force. It
has been with us now for some centuries, certainly since the break-
away from the Established Church. Even in the 18th century it
was being said that 'all being of one mould there is no reason that
some should have so much and others so little'. The political claim

1

to equality has led to at least two major revolutions — the French
and the Russian. In this placid and slow-moving country it has
brought about political equality in the sense that everyone above
the age of 18 may now choose whom he or she wishes politically
to govern the country. Political equality in its turn must inevitably
lead to a demand for economic equality — equality in wealth and
income. I will cite two quotations. First, de Toqueville: Men, once
they are equal in some respects, 'must come in the end to be equal
upon all'. Second, Henry Sidgwick, writing in 1907 of equality:

> . . . this mode of apportioning the means of happiness is likely to produce
> more happiness on the whole, not only because men have a disinterested
> aversion to unreason, but still more because they have an aversion to any
> kind of inferiority to others (which is much intensified when the inferi-
> ority seems unreasonable). This latter feeling is so strong that it often
> prevails in spite of obvious claims of desert; and it may even be sometimes
> expedient that it should so prevail.

I shall have occasion to revert to the quotation. Meanwhile, let us
just note that the tide towards equality, economic as well as political, is strong and, as far as one can foresee, is irreversible. Inequality of all sorts has lost its legitimacy. To say this is not to praise it
or to regret it; it is just realistically to observe a given fact of life.
    And yet, despite the power of the tide, economic inequality
persists. It clearly persists in capitalist countries, where the means
of production are still, up to a point anyhow, privately owned and
where therefore inequality of wealth makes for and compounds
inequality in income from work. But economic inequality persists
also — I think 'persist' is the right word — in communist countries,
where the means of production have passed into the hands of the
state. Marx distinguished between two phases of communism: a
first phase which still bore the birthmark of the preceding capitalist phase and in which each would be paid according to his work;
and a second phase in which communism and, with it, industrialisation had come to full flower, the forces of production would be
mobilised on behalf of society as a whole, and each could be paid
according to his need. It would be true to say that no communist
society has yet entered the second phase. Each is still in the first
phase in which payment is according to work rather than according to need, though it would be probably true to add that the
resulting inequalities in income from work are less in newer communist countries such as China, Cuba and North Korea than in
older ones. Be that as it may, the universal phenomenon, universal
in the sense of being common to both capitalist and communist

countries, is inequality in income from work. There is perhaps one exception to this generalisation — in the kibbuzim of Israel. There, as I understand it, payment is according to need — age, number of children, and so on — and not according to work, so that a leader may be paid less than other members of the kibbuz. This is perhaps a relic of the Menshevik phase in the evolution of communism. Interesting though it is, it is small in relation to the world picture which I have painted — namely, universal inequality in income from work despite the abolition in, let us say half the world, of private ownership in the means of production. For this reason I am confining this talk to inequality of income and not stretching it to include inequality of wealth. For the question to be answered is: how is this universality in the inequality of income to be explained? What is its justification? And if it has a justification how is this justification to be maintained against the tide towards equality in all things?

Let us first ask ourselves how far inequality is necessary for economic growth or efficiency. I suppose that economically the fastest growing countries in the world today are the oil-producing countries. I have spent the last two and a half years or so living in two of them. In both, the state is responsible for something like 75% of the gross domestic product. In both, the oil industry is nationalised and the basic means of production — oil and the capital equipment to extract and dispose of oil — can be said to be publicly owned. Revenues from oil accrue in the first instance to the state. From the state they flow downwards — to civil servants, to managers of state-owned undertakings, possibly to private owners of businesses which may have been established by themselves or which may have been started by the state but which the state has decided to hive off. A new middle class is arising — a middle class which is not the initiator of industrialisation as was the case in this country but which is the beneficiary of industrialisation started by the state. From this new middle class the revenues flow down farther — to the workers; but as they flow farther down, particularly to the unskilled, so they flow with diminished force. Indeed, the increase in the price of oil can be said to have had two consequences for the oil-producing countries. First, it has accelerated the rate of inflation because of the increased revenues at the disposal of the state; second, it has increased the disparity in incomes between rich and poor because of the weakening influence of state spending as it flows downwards. Anybody who has witnessed this growing disparity cannot but be appalled at the greed and the rapacity which it engenders.

Now there is no automatic economic mechanism to change or reverse this situation. There is no economic reason why this situation should not be self-perpetuating. The new middle class, thanks in part to rising income, in part to the tightness of family ties and its greater ability to educate its sons, could prolong itself unto the third and fourth generation, with disparities in income maintained, if not enlarged, in its favour. There is only one factor which could change this situation, and that is an act of political will. The exercise of that will is not easy. The main means of reducing disparities in income is through taxation, but the tax-collecting machinery is rudimentary. For the rest the prices of consumer goods can be subsidised and certain services can be rendered free — education and medical care, for example. But these are principally ways of helping the poor while also incidentally helping the rich; they do not therefore necessarily reduce differences in income.

The conclusion I draw from this account of contemporary developments in some of the world's most dynamic countries is that inequality in income is not the cause of the dynamism; it is the product of the dynamism. The inequalities could be narrowed, up to a point anyhow, without adverse effects on the rate of economic growth.

Clearly, I have to ask myself whether a similar situation did not obtain in my own country in its industrial heyday. And I am forced to the conclusion that it did. The new wealth of the Industrial Revolution was associated with a new middle class. That wealth was slow to flow downwards to the working class. But the disparity in income was not the cause of the new wealth; it was the outcome of the new wealth. And it was political pressure and political will that caused the disparity ultimately to be narrowed. In short, I am putting forward the thesis that inequalities in income are the result of a given set of historical conditions rather than of any particular economic rationale; and the degree of inequality is as a result generally defended on the ground of historic convention rather than on any other basis.

Having said that, I have to agree — as, I think, would most people — that there is a case for inequality. The main justification for inequality, as I see it, is that society is organised in a number of pyramids, different levels in each pyramid entailing different degrees of responsibility, these different degrees of responsibility requiring in their turn different degrees of capability. It seems reasonable to say that to induce people to accept a higher degree

of responsibility they should be paid a higher reward. But that
generalisation does not tell us how much higher the reward should
be. Much will depend on the ideological background from which a
person comes. A Chinese manager, for example, going to the
Soviet Union to occupy a position of responsibility similar to that
which he had occupied in China would be staggered at the higher
differential he would receive and probably appalled. A Russian
manager going similarly to the United States would be even more
staggered and would also be appalled. And I can tell you the story
of an Israeli friend of mine who had been leader of a semi-govern-
mental organisation earning less than those whom he supervised
for the simple reason that they had children and were paid accordingly and he had none. From Israel he went to the United States
to work for General Electric. Every three months an assessor
would come round to assess his work and because of the excel-
lence of his performance each quarter his salary was raised. This
was something my Israeli friend simply did not understand. He did
not want the money and thought the whole process silly and unnecessary. He changed his mind only when his wife gave birth to
a child and his desires immediately became unlimited.

Let me try and recapitulate: I have been trying to make two
simple points. First, while the inequality we have is an outcome of
history, a degree of inequality is inescapable. Indeed, one could
turn Sidgwick on his head and say that, just as people have a 'dis-
interested aversion' to the unreason of inequality, so also they
have an interested 'aversion' to complete equality — they want
something special for their own children or something to denote
their own achievement. Sidgwick's own assertion and its opposite
are paradoxically both valid, such is the complexity of human
nature. Second, there is no set of differentials denoting a univer-
sally ideal degree of inequality. Each society will have its own
degree of inequality dependent upon its history and an ideology
stretching back some length in time. There have been innumerable empirical researches attempting to measure whether inequality in incomes in this country has increased or decreased —
the latest one, that of the Royal Commission on the Distribution
of Incomes, suggesting that there has for some time been little
movement. I have nothing against such researches. But to have
real meaning they should imply not only a starting point but also
a finishing point. And the finishing point must be either complete
equality — which is unrealistic — or some ideal standard of inequality against which the movement can be measured. Let us be

clear that there is no such ideal standard. It would be wise, however, in seeking to diminish inequality, to be aware of the effects
of what we are doing. What have been the psychological and social
effects of a decrease in the inequality of incomes? Here, it seems
to me, the researches have been scanty and we remain in a state of
blissful ignorance. We do not really know.

Let us consider how incomes from work are currently determined in this country. The members of an industrial society may
be broadly divided into managers and managed. The managers, in
so far as they are executive members of a board of directors, determine their own salaries, subject to the approval of the non-executive
members, if there are any. In determining them they have an eye,
in part to the levels obtaining beneath them, in part to the levels
obtaining in other companies about which they are informed by
consultants. Consultants increasingly circulate salary surveys, and
there are some consultants who have begun to circulate international surveys of managerial salaries. The end result could well
be that managerial salaries could follow those of the highest pay-
ing country, when it is in fact by no means clear that industrial
managers are all that internationally mobile. I suspect that some
of the professions — doctors and academics — are more internationally mobile than industrial managers. Be that as it may,
managerial salaries in the private sector are then taken into account
by review bodies in making recommendations about top pay in
nationalised industries and in the Civil Service. All hell is then let
loose and the government is placed in a situation of acute embar-
rassment. It will be seen that the whole process is circular, one
company following another, possibly following another country,
the public sector following the private sector, and there is a general
state of dissatisfaction.

So much for the managers. Let us turn to the managed, who are
increasingly organised, the organisations now extending a considerable way up the managerial scale. Where there is organisation there
is potential power, an aspect of life left out of account in classical
economics. The extent to which the power will be pressed will
depend in part on the personality of the organisation's leader.
Where it is pressed it will then be pressed by others, either in a
pursuit for equality or in an attempt to maintain an inherited inequality. Coal miners will be followed by electricity workers,
electricity workers by railwaymen, and so on. The fact that one
organisation follows another is evidence of some dissatisfaction.
Where the dissatisfaction is minor it would not matter; but in

the two cases I have cited — top incomes in the public sector
following top incomes in the private sector, and railwaymen
following coal miners — the dissatisfaction is not minor; it is
patently major. And it is not abated by the fact of higher taxation
on higher incomes; for incomes net of tax are invisible, whereas
the gross incomes are visible.

The dissatisfaction arises because in the determination of the
incomes of both managers and managed there is an element of
power. In the case of, at any rate, some managers the power lies
in the fact that incomes are, up to a point, unilaterally determined;
and in the case of the managed it arises from the power of organisation. The resulting inequalities are then rejected as unreasonable.
To quote once again Sidgwick: '. . . men . . . have an aversion to
any kind of inferiority to others (which is much intensified when
the inferiority seems unreasonable)'. The problem then, if we
assume, as I do, that a degree of inequality is inevitable and desirable because it conforms with certain basic requirements of human
nature, is to find that particular degree of inequality which com-
mends itself to reason and on that ground is acceptable.

You may well ask: Is this at all feasible? And nobody can be
certain of the answer. All we know is that within individual undertakings the use of certain job evaluation techniques has made the
ranking of employees, and the different levels of pay associated
with different ranks, more acceptable than before. There is no
inherent reason therefore why the use of the same techniques
should not be extended across different undertakings and indeed
across different industries. For example, the most plausible theory
I have read about differences in the pay of managers in different
companies is that by H. Simon, in the United States. His theory
rests on one fact — namely, that there is a limit to the number of
sub-managers which any one manager can control — and on one
probability — namely, that there is a customary, though arbitrary,
ratio between the pay of a manager and that of a sub-manager. It
follows that the larger the company the greater the number of
managerial tiers; the greater the base of the pyramid, the greater
the height, and therefore the more the pay of the top manager. As
I say, the theory is plausible, but, if the justification for inequality
is responsibility, is it true that the responsibility carried by the top
manager of company A is twice that carried by the top manager of
company B, half its size, and therefore warrants twice the pay? I
do not know, but I would like the question put to the test.

True, the use of job evaluation techniques may be complicated

by the pull of the market, particularly the international market.
Take, for example, an airline pilot. The content of his job may
not be as great as that of a supervising manager; but he commands
for his skill an international market which his more home-bound
manager does not. Some compromise might need to be effected
therefore between the income indicated by job content and that
indicated by the command of an international market.

Despite these difficulties we have to do something for we have
to recognise that we are faced with a dilemma. On the one hand
the inequalities resulting from the manner in which society now
operates are not accepted. On the other hand, we seem to be
drifting blindly towards an equality which could be equally
rejected as unreasonable. We have consciously to chart a course
between the two. This to me is the main purpose of an incomes
policy.

I very much regret the fact that an incomes policy has come to
be spoken of solely in terms of the problem of inflation. I am one
of those who believe that an incomes policy can provide something
of an answer to the problem of inflation, though not in isolation.
But it is not with inflation that I am today concerned. I am concerned with something deeper. I am concerned with the inevita-
bility of a degree of inequality, a degree different from the one we
have, and with the need therefore to make that degree intelligible
to reason, so that society can cohere better together. That is the
real case for an incomes policy.

At the moment we have an incomes policy prescribing a flat
rate increase of £6 a week for incomes below £8,500 a year. Let
us suppose that this policy lasts for an entire year, what then? As
a result of the policy relative incomes will be different from what
they otherwise would have been; inequalities will have been diminished. If the policy is then entirely abandoned there will be a
rush to restore the preceding relationships, the preceding inequalities. From the national standpoint this would be undesirable, for
the rush would entail a new acceleration of the rate of inflation,
assuming it by then to have abated. From the standpoint of an
egalitarian it would equally be undesirable, for the rush would un-
do much that will have been done in the intervening year towards
reducing inequality. I think it inevitable therefore that the policy
in one form or another will continue.

Clearly, I cannot foretell the precise form in which it will
continue. All I can do is to list certain criteria to which it should
have regard. I would name three. First, it should lean, as now, in

favour of the lower incomes, though clearly less rigidly than now; too abrupt a departure from this bias would be unacceptable. Second, it should take account of the rate at which the country in general is generating an increase in income, for it is against this background that increases in individual incomes have to be seen. Third and last, it should endeavour to ground in reason differences in income both within the hierarchy of a particular firm or industry and across different industries, and an important part of that reason should be the content of the job done.

I would like to conclude with an appeal to economists. Let them end this arid debate between the champions of an incomes policy and the champions of a monetary policy. The debate is over. We have an incomes policy, and for the reasons I have given we are stuck with it, whether we like it or not. Let economists then bend their minds, if need be in concert with other social scientists, to the constructive, needed and admittedly difficult task of analysing and assessing the degree of inequality which might commend itself to the reason of the very reasonable people of this particular country.

D. A. REISMAN
University of Surrey

2 Social justice and macroeconomic policy: the case of J K Galbraith*

John Kenneth Galbraith was an early convert to Keynesian ideas, partly under the influence of Alvin Hansen at Harvard (where Galbraith was appointed Instructor in 1933), and partly because of the success of Roosevelt's 'New Deal' (a case in point of government spending in excess of tax revenues in order to combat depression). In 1937-8 Galbraith even came to England on a Social Science Research Council Fellowship to meet Keynes (who was then unfortunately suffering from a heart attack, but whom he later met in Washington during the War) and spent a year studying with Keynes' disciples.

Galbraith is, however, a Keynesian with a difference. He recognises that policies to combat recession and inflation by manipulating the level of aggregate demand may be frustrated by the new nature of macroeconomic disequilibrium induced in the modern economy by the mature corporation and the large trade union. Because of the fact that the world of large organisations (what Galbraith calls the 'planning system') is prone to instability and resistant to the general market regulation favoured by Keynes, he believes that direct controls on wages and prices must, and will, become an essential part of the interventionist's tool kit. Such

* I would like to thank Professor Galbraith for his interest and encouragement, and in particular for his helpful comments on an earlier draft of this paper. Any errors and omissions remain, of course, strictly my own responsibility.

10

controls underline the microeconomic origins of macroeconomic instability, make intervention specific as well as general, and permit the choice of a second policy objective, social justice, alongside stabilisation.

All policy means choice of objectives and intervention in markets. Galbraith argues that since the choice of stabilisation as a goal involves a value judgement there is no reason to suppose the choice of social justice as an additional aim to be less justifiable in itself. He is also aware, however, that more goals necessitate the use of more policy instruments.

In this paper our plan of campaign will be as follows: We will first show why the existence of the planning system makes macroeconomic instability endemic to the modern economy, then explain why the orthodox tools of macroeconomic policy (monetary and fiscal) are inadequate to deal with the situation, and then discuss the case for (and nature of) a prices and incomes policy. We will conclude by pointing out what we consider to be the main flaws in Galbraith's important contribution to the sociology of macroeconomics.

Macroeconomic stability is essential to the large corporation (which must be able to forecast future levels of the national income as a precondition for forecasting future levels of specific demand for its own product). So is the autonomy of its decision-makers. Yet, paradoxically, the planning system itself is a source of macroeconomic instability and a cause of increased state intervention in economic activity. Consider first the case of a recession and then the case of a period of inflation.

(i) In a recession there is unemployment of inputs due to a deficiency in effective demand for output, and typically the cause is oversaving: income earned by households is not being fully spent on consumer goods, and firms are not anxious voluntarily to invest the equivalent of the amount saved.

Among small-scale price-takers (i.e. in what Galbraith calls the 'market system') such oversaving is unlikely. Firms are little, their savings minimal, and any rise in disposable incomes likely soon to be translated into a rise in investment. If the small firm does save without converting profits into plant, such funds will be deposited in a bank and made available to other entrepreneurs; and both savers and borrowers will be sensitive to changes in interest rates. Moreover, if savings do exceed investment in a freely competitive economy, then wages and prices will fall (while output and employment will not), a process which will cause the frugal to save less out of declining incomes while stimulating those on fixed incomes to consume more. Hence, in the market system (and albeit subject in practice to rigidities such as the reluctance of wages and prices in the short-run to fall), self-stabilising mechanisms exist, Say's Law eventually obtains, and there is no possibility of a protracted shortfall of total demand.

We live in a dual economy, however; and alongside the market system (and approximately equal to it as a percentage of the GNP) exists the planning system, which is inherently unstable. In the modern economy, the preponderant share of savings is corporate, and there is no mechanism by which desired corporate savings and desired corporate investment will automatically be equated. Indeed, planners actually prefer to have too much rather than too little savings, since this guarantees them autonomy from nosy lenders and also means that they will be able rapidly to substitute capital for labour should the need arise (after all, 'machines do not go on strike'[1]). Decision-makers, moreover, are insensitive to the rate of interest since the firm is insulated from the capital market: savings and investment are planned, and the corporation has a policy of financing growth out of internal sources of funds. Even dividends paid to keep shareholders passive tend to be deflationary, since rich rentiers are more likely to save than to spend on consumption.

Recession is hence a real danger in an affluent society. Savings may be meagre in poor countries but they are more than ample in the capital-rich countries of the West. Here, 'not a shortage of savings but a recession resulting from the failure to use all available savings is the spectre that haunts all policy makers. For investment to exceed savings, at least in peacetime, is thought exceptional'[2] . Moreover, in the planning system (unlike the market system), recession touched off by a deficiency of aggregate demand is not self-correcting and can become cumulative. In a recession the large corporation notices that its plant is not fully employed and cuts back on or postpones further investment, thereby making the depression worse. And the large corporation does not in any case meet a fall in demand by cutting wages and prices (which are administered and inflexible because of unions and oligopolistic conventions) but instead reduces employment and output once it has recognised the permanence of stocks of unwanted *ex post* investment that have piled up. To make matters worse, demand based on persuasion and not physical need is unreliable: when incomes fall consumers are hence very likely to cut their spending on unnecessary luxuries, thereby causing the depression to deepen and to spread to the market system.

(ii) In a period of inflation, there is buoyancy of demand in the economy, abundant spending and a sustained rise in prices.

In the market system, if demand exceeds supply, then the usual tools of monetary and fiscal policy can be applied, reducing demand until prices cease to rise. Unions complicate the picture, but they are typically absent from the market system (consider the examples of American agriculture or petty retailing), and where they exist they are moderate in their demands (since they know the price-taker cannot absorb higher wages through higher prices, and that unemployment is likely to result where the entrepreneur fails in his vociferous resistance to the union's claims). In any case, unions in the market system often tend towards passivity so long as the cost-of-living index is not rising, as it will not be so long as the level of total demand is under control.

In the planning system, on the other hand, firms do have power in their respective markets, and so in consequence do unions. The latter push for and obtain pay above the level that would have been set by supply and demand and risk no unemployment, since the modern corporation is able to pass on a wage rise in excess of productivity gains via a rise in the price of final output (at the expense of the private consumer or the powerless firm in the market system) or through a reduction in distributed profits (at the expense of the shareholders). The specialists (or 'technostructure') who are collectively the corporate decision-makers have no compunctions about exporting inflation, either to the public at large or to the firm's own capitalists (the technostructure is keen to maximise its own job-satisfaction, security and growth, but hardly the profits of the firm, in which the man on a salary does not share). Higher prices or lower profits, of course, are not conducive to security and growth, but neither is a prolonged strike. A strike means that production is disrupted, time wasted, the prestige of the technostructure tarnished, and an atmosphere of conflict created which may reduce future worker identification with the goals of the corporation.

Because the technostructure has the power to export inflation to other sectors of the economy, traditional class antagonisms and militancy have been replaced by a new climate of 'mellowness in collective bargaining. The employer who cannot get along with his union has become hopelessly *déclassé*. He is tactfully but firmly excluded from the list of after-luncheon speakers; he must himself listen to the modern hero, the man who has negotiated twenty contracts but never had a strike'[3]. One should not be misled by the 'ceremonial insult'[4] which usually accompanies collective bargaining: it is just for show. A better index of the excellent relations between labour and management that obtain in the new industrial state is the decline of trade-union membership[5]. After all, decision-makers on a salary as well as workers on a wage can share in the gains from cost-push inflation that arise in the planning system.

Of course, management would resist an excessive wage-claim if it seriously expected a substantial drop in the supply of internally generated funds so essential to corporate planning to result; but such a situation is unlikely in view of Galbraith's opinion that modern salesmanship and market manipulation are so effective that the mature corporation can set both the price of the product and the quantity sold. Clearly, if the giant firm dominates and controls the markets in which it trades, then it need not face a downward-sloping demand curve. A higher price need not lead to loss of sales, and hence the possibility of having to absorb higher wages through lower retained earnings is extremely remote.

Again, management would offer countervailing power to the union in a period of recession. When inflation exists, employers and unions form a sort of unholy alliance, a massive monolithic locus of original power, and tacitly collude to pass the burden of a wage-rise on to vulnerable groups without any countervailing power at all. The advantage of recession is that it keeps the two sides of industry in opposition and thus ensures the continuance of the precarious balance between them. Class-conflict rather than compatibility of interests, under-full rather than full employment, appear to be the true public interest. Yet this situation too is unlikely in view of the public commitment, in the post-Keynesian era, to maintain full employment and to stabilise the level of aggregate demand. Try as we may, it is not easy to escape from the morass of conciliation.

The traditional tools of macroeconomic policy are monetary and fiscal policy. Both are aimed at regulating the level of total demand, but both have failed to deal adequately with the problem of inflation. It will be useful to examine why this has been so.

(i) The monetary problem is 'a continuing high demand for bank loans which if granted add to bank deposits and therewith the money supply. Then when the deposit money so created is spent, the resulting demand pulls up prices'[6]. Hence, by monetary policy we mean manipulation of the supply of funds available for borrowing from banks and of the rates of interest at which that borrowing takes place.

Unfortunately, central bank intervention to restrict the money supply or raise interest rates will little affect the large corporation. Cut off from the uncertainties and costs of the market, it minimises its dependence on borrowed funds and ploughs back earnings in order to gain financial independence. And even if it is forced to borrow, the large firm is able to pass on a rise in interest rates to its customers (not being a profit-maximiser, it has substantial unliquidated gains); and in such a case interest-rate policy, aimed at discouraging demand-pull, can be a positive encouragement to cost-push inflation. Clearly, such interest-insensitivity frustrates monetary policy.

The small operator in the market system, on the other hand, will, being a persistent borrower, be hard hit by rising interest rates. Farmers and small retailers have little internal funds and are dependent on outside sources of savings. Being price-takers rather than price-setters, they cannot pass the higher cost on to the consumer. And it is not only interest-rate policy that favours the strong at the expense of the weak. Monetary policy operating through credit-restraint forces banks and other lenders to discriminate between applicants for a limited quantity of money; and the large corporation such as General Motors (a prime borrower with an excellent credit-rating) will always be preferred to the small self-employed potter or the secretary anxious to open a boutique.

Monetary policy thus has undesirable directional effects. It victimises the market system (the weak) to the benefit of the planning system (the strong), an injustice compounded by the recollection of the central role played by the planning system in the generation of our modern inflation in any case. Monetary policy promotes sectoral inequalities of income and development, and also retards many socially-desirable undertakings (in America, for example, both the housing industry and the local authorities have a high propensity to borrow). Indeed, precisely because of these injustices monetary policy is seldom rigorously applied, since the severity of its application has had and will have to be tempered by social and humanitarian considerations: 'It will be easy to see why monetary policy is regarded with equanimity and even approval by larger and stronger firms. Unless applied with severity over time it does not appreciably affect them . . . Before the large volume investment spending of the larger and more powerful firms is affected, a severe squeeze will ordinarily be placed on the capital requirements of small-scale firms . . . This will set severe limits on the rigour with which the policy may be pursued. For, apart from the social aspects of a policy which denies growth to the numerous and small and favours the large and the powerful, farmers and small businessmen are not without political influence'[7].

Monetary policy, moreover, is a blunt and dangerous instrument, and it is nonsense to speak (as the Nixon Administration did in 1969) of using it for 'fine-tuning': 'One could as well speak of fine-tuning a major Mississippi flood . . . The policy being pursued was called the 'game plan' for defeating inflation. There had been no game quite like it since the Rose Bowl of 1929 when Roy Riegels ran 75 yards towards the wrong goal'[8]. The effects of monetary policy are unpredictable and uncertain (an overly-restrictive set of measures could well loose a major depression by accident),[9] and can be perverse: a policy intended to use rising interest rates as a trick to convert speculators into firm holders of debt, for example, assumes that they will not notice the probability of such mouse-trapping until after they have bought the debt, and it is unlikely that they are such cretins.[10]

In short, monetary policy has undesirable distributional effects and is besides 'palpable failure'[11]. Clearly, it is not a suitable tool to use in the war on inflation, except perhaps in the odd-short-run crisis (in 1974, for example, Galbraith advised that 'money must for now be kept tight').[12] Normally, however, the authorities should aim at a stable and permanently low level of the rate of interest. Stable rates (and this implies a fixed structure of rates) are desirable, being as attractive to lenders as high rates because of the diminished risk of capital loss.[13] Low rates are desirable since they stimulate borrowing by the weak and have a welcome redistributive effect (borrowers generally 'have less money than lenders').[14] Once stable and low rates of interest are set, control of the price and quantity of money should then cease to be a tool of macroeconomic policy.

(ii) The term fiscal policy refers to government expenditure, taxation, and to the balance between them (the annual budget).

Consider first government expenditure. Galbraith, following Keynes, believes that this in a period of depression should be substantially increased in order to raise the level of aggregate demand, offset excess savings, and create jobs for the unemployed (both directly and through the multiplier process). However, Galbraith, and this Keynes did not observe, identifies here a ratchet effect which impedes an analogous contraction in total demand by means of a reduction in government expenditure in a period of inflation: 'Like private consumption, any new public service quickly becomes a part of the accustomed standard of living. Once given, support to schools or hospitals or parks or public transportation cannot be readily withdrawn'.[15]

Galbraith welcomes this asymmetry. The public services are, after all, so starved of funds that it is always right to increase them and never right to decrease them. Moreover, it is important to disaggregate any potential cuts in government spending to see exactly where the incidence of stabilisation policy falls before such cuts are recommended.

The fact is that in America much of public expenditure is orientated towards military procurement and defence-related industries, and it would be deemed unpatriotic for a politician to suggest that military spending be cut as part of the fight against inflation. The state bureaucracy and the powerful technostructure too will join forces to oppose any cuts which imperil their promotion prospects and forecasts of future demand, or which reduce public support for technological advance (here again we encounter the close lines that exist between microeconomics and macroeconomics). As a result, reductions in government expenditure favour (or hurt least) the planning system: 'The power of the planning system in the community has also won immunity for public expenditures important to itself — highways, industrial research, rescue loans, national defense. They have the sanction of a higher public purpose'.[16] This means that reductions in government expenditure are concentrated in the field of welfare, housing and social services in general; and these are even now near the minimum level the community regards as tolerable (partly because of the outdated economic theology of laissez-faire, partly because of the absence of want-creation in the public sector). Since in a period of inflation the public services are even worse off than usual (because public pay scales tend to lag behind those in the private sector), it is clearly not in the national interest to sacrifice social policy to fiscal policy.

Of course, it could be argued that a true perception of the nature of the Cold War (it is over) and of the power of bureaucracies state and corporate (it is excessive) might allow intelligent and courageous politicians to reduce government spending in such a way as to penalise the military and the planning system rather than the welfare state. Yet, while true perception is always preferable to false consciousness, a reduction in public expenditure remains undesirable. Any cuts in defence spending must be matched by alternative support to the planning system in order to finance technologically sophisticated areas of research and development that are in the public interest (such as the exploration of space or of the sea-bed; or the study of how to alter the world's weather) but would not otherwise be commercially viable. And even if public support to the planning system were to be reduced, there are many valuable projects in the state sector (medical care, law enforcement or support to the arts, for example) which are at present painfully short of funds.

Public expenditure must be governed by public needs; and there is no assurance, for political and social reasons, that such spending will be at the optimal level from the point of view of aggregate demand. Public expenditure can be increased in a recession; but Galbraith is adamant that it must not be reduced as part of a strategy to combat inflation.

Consider now the case of taxation. Here again we are confronted with the inelasticities of a 'one-way street'.[17] In a recession taxes should not be cut: the worst way to stimulate a depressed economy is to reduce taxes on the well-to-do in the hope that their increased spending will create jobs for the unemployed. Lower taxes are a rationalisation for selfishness and commodity hedonism at the expense of essential public services which help the poor and needy. What is needed in a recession is unemployment compensation, retraining and re-education schemes, even direct employment in the public sector,[18] and all of this costs money since coping with a recession is an expensive proposition. Galbraith hence had occasion in 1962 to warn President Kennedy against the persuasive arguments of the grand coalition between Keynesians and conservatives on the question of tax reduction: 'Money from tax reduction goes into the pockets of those who need it least; lower tax revenues will become a ceiling on spending'[19].

In a period of inflation, on the other hand, a rise in taxes operates as a valuable policy variable. An increase in taxation (possibly an increase so large as to promote a desirably deflationary budget surplus[20]) helps to reduce total demand (although once again fine-tuning is impossible and lags are a problem) and also has an effect identical to an increase in interest rates, namely reduction of borrowing: the higher taxes are, the less people can afford to borrow, and the less firms will want to expand capital in the face of falling demand for commodities. Income taxes, moreover, have the additional advantage of being discriminatory in their incidence, progressive and redistributive (whereas a straightforward rise in interest rates is not) and thus kill two birds with one stone: they help to stabilise the level of total demand (not least as a built-in stabiliser where nominal rates are unchanged) and act as a force for greater equality in society. The progressive bias could even be accentuated by an anti-inflation emergency surcharge of 10% on personal incomes of over $15,000 and of 20% on incomes of over $20,000. There is also a need to close tax loopholes: the present American tax system is an invitation to avoidance and it is only logical that the rich have become 'a bunch of dropouts from the Federal tax system'.[21]

To combat inflation, corporation tax should be raised; and (with the subsidiary aim of social engineering) indirect taxes should be mobilised as well. There could be a special purchase tax on luxuries; and, since rising energy and food prices have been cost-pushing up the average price index, there could be discriminatory taxation on commodities that waste energy (e.g. cars and air conditioners) and food (e.g. restaurant meals).[22]

In any case, high taxes help to compensate for the effects of cheap money and hence represent a hidden subsidy to borrowers (whom, as we have seen, Galbraith regards as the deserving poor).

Galbraith is hence a friend to taxation, which he recognises to be a useful means, both of deflating purchasing power and also of placing a discriminatory burden on the rich. Tax policy combines the fight against rising prices with the fight for narrowing differentials, but it is open to two important objections. One of these Galbraith accepts. The other he rejects.

The first objection, and the one Galbraith accepts, is that, although the burden of tax policy is more equal as between firms than the burden of monetary policy, it nonetheless distorts the economy towards the powerful. The planning system (unlike the market system) may be able to pass on the increase to the final consumer in the form of higher prices, and in such a case higher taxes actually feed the inflation.

The second objection, and the one Galbraith rejects, is that higher taxes act as a disincentive to initiative and effort. There is nowadays, Galbraith argues, a remarkable divorce of payment from incentive. The organisation man may complain bitterly that high taxes make him indifferent to promotion or hard work, but this is special pleading and the government ought not to take him at his word. The very arguments used with respect to motivation are out of date: 'Compulsion had an ancient association with land. Pecuniary motivation had a similar association with capital. Identification and adaptation are associated with the technostructure.'[23] At the nucleus of the planning system, group loyalty and professional ethics place strict limits on the technocrat's opportunity to vary the quantity of the work he performs. Besides, the highest paid jobs happen also to bring with them the greatest prestige, power and job-satisfaction, the greatest degree of identification with the organisation, the greatest opportunity to influence or adapt its purposes and policies, the greatest fringe benefits (such as more flexible hours, special dining facilities, expense accounts). The lowest paid jobs, on the other hand, are likely to be associated with boring work, alienation from decision-making, and a quite understandable obsession with the effort/income ratio. Clearly, regardless of the rate of taxes, money is not everything: 'To be an executive would still be far better than fitting bolts on the shop floor.'[24] If any group faces an upward-sloping supply curve of effort with respect to net pecuniary compensation, it is surely more likely to be the low paid than the affluent, the powerful and the job-satisfied.

There is another reason why a rise in taxes will not cause middle and higher income groups to substitute leisure for work, and this is the powerful income effect represented by promotion prospects. No organisation man would admit to his employer that he is not fully exerting himself because of insufficient pecuniary incentive: 'The typical business executive makes his way to the top by promotion over the heads of his fellows. He would endanger his chance for advancement if he were suspected of gold-bricking because of his resentment over his taxes. He is expected to give his best to his corporation, and usually be does'[25]. Discontent over reward does not mean disincentive to labour: 'Not even managers contend that pay has an incentive effect, for it is the pride of every executive that he puts forth his best regardless of pay. He would not possibly have it suggested that he graduate his effort or his exercise of intelligence to his compensation'.[26]

A rise in direct taxes, therefore, will have little disincentive effect because of the divorce between pay and exertion in modern large organisations. Unfortunately, servile politicians have been bamboozled by economists and organisation men into believing that present pay differentials are functionally necessary to ensure the performance of specific tasks calling for specific skills whose value is impersonally set by supply and demand. This is a fiction, however, as compensation in the planning system is determined, not by market valuation of productivity, but by tradition and position in the hierarchy of bureaucratic power. The men at the top of the scale have the power to fix their own remuneration, and it is hence (not surprisingly) excessively generous: 'There is no evidence and no reason to suppose that the supply of executive talent requires the stimulation of the present prices. The number of able and eager candidates is consistently large'.[27] A surplus clearly exists (since reduced remuneration would reduce neither the quantity supplied of skilled labour, nor its productivity); and in the interests both of anti-inflationary policy and social justice this surplus must be captured for society by progressive taxation.

Of the orthodox tools of stabilisation policy in a period of inflation, Galbraith rejects a rise in the rate of interest, control over the supply of money, or cuts in public spending; and is only really attracted by increases in direct taxation. Since the government's ability to raise levels of taxation is, however, for both economic and political reasons, rather circumscribed, this suggests that Galbraith is far from optimistic about the adequacy of aggregate demand policy to contain inflation. Moreover, not only does he find aggregate demand policy *inadequate*, he also finds it *undesirable* as a strategy for dealing with the problem of rising prices. His scepticism derives from the following arguments:

First, Galbraith regards as brutal and wasteful the theory that there is a trade-off between stable prices and full employment, with its implication that a nation can have one or the other but not both: 'Whoever made respectable economic policy a choice between such repellent alternatives had a bad upbringing and is obviously a very mean man. But so it is'[28] . Deflation reduces the level of demand for commodities (output which admittedly does not satisfy needs of any great urgency), but also creates unemployment and sacrifices security and growth; and it is possible that the cure is worse than the disease, not least for the politicians whose courageous but unpopular action in putting the brakes on the economy leads to their ultimate rejection by the electorate.[29]

Second, we must remind ourselves that monetary and fiscal policy are tools for dealing with demand-pull inflation, the variety that obtains in the market system. There, prices rise whenever total demand exceeds total supply, but not otherwise as total supply would then exceed total demand and prices would fall again to dispose of unsold output. In the planning system, however, most inflation is cost-push, where pay rises are not resisted by a technostructure able to pass the burden on to the consumer or back to the shareholder. In a world of corporate planning, collective bargaining and internal funds, monetary and fiscal measures are water off a duck's back; and the burden of deflation is likely to fall disproportionately on the small and the weak. Such is the problem of managing a dual economy: upon disaggregating we might find an economic success to be a social failure.

Third, and analogous to our second point, the existence of a dual labour force must be recognised, a labour-force divided into the more educated and the less educated. The only way to ensure full employment of the latter is to run the economy at a very high level of demand; but this in turn causes substantial competition for the scarce services of the former, a rapid rise in the wages of the highly qualified, and price inflation. Similarly, demand deflation will have to be very severe in its incidence on the unskilled before it has any effect of consequence on the best trained. The pool of unemployed that is created when demand is deflated is not a random cross-section of the population but tends to reflect excessively the marginal and the vulnerable; and it is quite simply socially unjust to sack Tom (a poor uneducated young urban black from a broken home) for the sake of Dick and Harry, even if Tom is given unemployment compensation or retrained at public expense.

Fourth, the Phillips curve may yield bad predictions. The result of deflation has, on occasion, been stagflation, a situation which combines 'a politically unacceptable level of unemployment with a socially damaging rate of inflation. This is now being accomplished in the United States, and with no great effort'.[30] Clearly, a policy which combines unemployment with rising wages and prices rather than trading more of the former for less of the latter produces the worst, not the best, of possible worlds.

Demand deflation must be approached with caution, therefore. Yet inflation cannot be tolerated, since it is without doubt 'a hideously unfair thing':[31] 'The modern inflation is not neutral. Because of its inevitable identification with economic strength, it is inequitable, regressive, and reactionary'.[32] Strong unions, giant corporations and the fast on their feet benefit, while weak unions, small firms, pensioners, civil servants, savers, all those without effective bargaining power lag behind. Such injustice must be brought to an end, and there is but one solution: we must sacrifice our limping market economy (and the myth that it is 'free') and institute a system of direct governmental controls on pay and prices. Such controls are inescapable: 'I see no alternative, no other way of reconciling high employment with price stability'.[33]

Governments on both sides of the Atlantic having already recognised the inevitable, the question is no longer whether such controls are good or bad, simply what form they will take. On this Galbraith, who was Assistant Administrator in the wartime Office of Price Administration from 1941 to 1943 and had a nationwide staff of up to 16,000 under his direction, is strikingly well qualified to speak: 'I am not without experience in the practical side of price control or in the difficulties involved. During the Second World War, price control was under my direction from its inception until mid-1943. No one else, I suppose, has ever fixed so many prices'.[34] Specifically, Galbraith recommends that a prices and incomes policy be formulated along the following lines.

First the introduction of guidelines should be preceded by a six months freeze on all pay and prices to break the structure of inflationary expectations, both of spenders (whose increased confidence in the currency means they 'will not be moved to reduce current savings or spend past savings'[35]) and of unions (who will eschew escalation clauses and come to see that collective bargaining can and must be on the assumption of a stable cost of living).

Second, the policy should be one of 'supervised self-regulation'[36] which means it should be worked out by a tripartite commission representing all sides of industry (labour, management, the public). The recommendations of this commission should be legally enforceable since a voluntary incomes policy has little chance of winning adequate cooperation.

Third, the policy should not be temporary but permanent. Expectations of its relaxation will not be conducive to its success, and moreover the problem with which it must deal is permanent.

Fourth, and because controls will only succeed if they have the cooperation of the worker and the confidence of the consumer, they must be both comprehensive and integrated into the whole complex of government policy measures (including tax policy). Clearly, 'one cannot have wage stabilization unless living costs, profits, and executive compensation are also stable'.[37]

Fifth, incomes should be planned and in such a way as to narrow the gap between the rich and the poor. Galbraith believes that 'the most general and urgent problem of the modern economy is not the production of goods but the distribution of its income'[38] ; and argues that since power rather than productivity is at the basis of the present pay structure, countervailing power must be exercised to narrow rather than freeze differentials. The lower paid are nowadays less willing to tolerate the lower standards of living and the highly stratified pay structures that they found acceptable in the past; and such perceptions of relative rather than merely absolute deprivation would lead to a perpetual cycle of embittered leapfrogging were the government not to step in and redistribute opportunities to participate in the common product.[39] Now that 'economic policy has become an aspect of politics'[40], Galbraith is confident that in the near future the 'movement toward a more consciously egalitarian income distribution will become an indispensable aspect of successful economic policy'.[41]

Sixth, controls should not apply to the market system: small firms (say, those employing less than 1,000 workers) should be exempt, as should all wage bargains not covered by collective bargaining contracts. Controls should apply only to the planning system, and for that reason it cannot be said that they interfere with the freedom of markets: 'The policy interferes with markets in which the interference of unions and corporations is already plenary. It fixes in the public interest prices that are already fixed'[42]. Since controls are to operate only in markets dominated by giant corporations and strong unions, they need not, in practice, be an exceptional administrative burden: 'In the United States only a few hundred unions and around a thousand corporations need to be touched'[43]. Moreover, modern imperfect competition has made price controls easier to implement than is generally imagined, since prices in oligopolistic markets tend even without regulation to be rigid and 'it is relatively easy to fix prices that are already fixed.'[44]

Dismemberment of the planning system is not a realistic proposal since great corporations as well as powerful unions would have to be broken up, a process that could prove fatal to technological advance and other economies of large scale. The alternative, if the economy is not to experience cost-push inflation, is for pay and prices in the planning system to be fixed by a handful of public sector bureaucrats rather than a handful of private sector technocrats. Yet academic economists have regrettably neglected to provide professional guidance to bureaucrats and politicians on how to plan earnings structures so as to serve the public purpose: 'There is little discussion of controls in the universities', Galbraith complains, because of a 'normal innocent commitment to intellectual obsolescence.'[45]

Such intellectual obsolescence is deplorable. Even economists must face the frightening fact that 'the age of Keynesian economics is now over; the macroeconomic revolution in fiscal and monetary management which we owe to Keynes has run foul of the microeconomic revolution in trade union and corporate power'[46]. New problems exist. They demand new solutions.

Galbraith's contribution is valuable. He has stressed not just the directional effects of inflation but the directional effects of monetary and fiscal policy as well, has shown that it is impossible for macroeconomic policy to be neutral as between social classes and groups, and has introduced a humanistic element into discussions on economic stability through his refusal to treat people as numbers, as fuel for a hungry computer. Galbraith has shown that centralised planning and price-fixing already exist in a large section of the economy, and has given valuable advice to public decision-makers on how too to fix pay and prices, but so as to combine social justice with price stability. Such planning of pay and prices indeed is an efficient, as well as an equitable, tool: aggregate demand policies have demonstrably failed to halt inflation (notably cost-push inflation in the planning system), and even if they did so would only purchase stability at the cost of employment and growth.

There are, however, several important gaps in Galbraith's discussion of macroeconomic policy. First, the reality that union leaders and management do still indulge in strikes and confrontation, and the existence of class conflict and even accelerating militancy, tend to suggest either that the workers are unaware of the climate of industrial harmony that prevails in the Age of Aquarius, or that there are strict limitations on the corporation's power to absorb wage rises by passing them forward to the consumer or backward to the shareholder. Even in Galbraith's own model management would resist wage-claims if the corporation is unable to raise the price of the final product (lest, say, the rise disturb the tacit collusion of a sleepy oligopolistic market; lest the rise cause the consumer to shift brands where each firm has a different degree of labour-intensity and hence raises its price by a different amount; or lest the rise in price cause the consumer to substitute an alternative product altogether, assuming the existence of a high cross-elasticity of demand). Again, management might also resist wage-claims where they cannot pass the increased burden back to the shareholder (the case where the owners are not mere coupon-clippers but take an active interest in the profits of their corporation; or where managers themselves have large blocs of shares). Nor should we forget that the security and growth of the corporation (the goals of its salaried technostructure who make its crucial decisions) depend on a large pool of profits available to be reinvested, not to be handed out in pay-packets. In short, countervailing power may not be dead after all: the large corporation might not always cave in to union pressures, and might resist just as fiercely as the small shopkeeper or the farmer in the market system.

Second, Galbraith recognises that even pay and price controls will only succeed if aggregate demand policies exist so as to equate total demand with total supply. Yet he also rejects out of hand the use of monetary policy, a recommendation which could lead to a wildly inflationary flood of borrowing and spending. Such a flood could naturally be curbed by credit-rationing, where the banks are requested by the state to gear lending to the needs of society as defined by a table of priorities; but Galbraith does not advocate the use of the banking system as an arm of national economic planning (and would certainly antagonise monetarists even more were he to have done so). As for fiscal policy, he is perhaps unwise not to countenance any reductions in public spending (however desirable parks and schools may be in their own right); and does not explain what will happen in the long run in a cyclically dominated economy if public spending always rises in the down-swing but never falls in the up-swing. He is left with one orthodox weapon in the fight against inflation, tax policy, and this may prove inadequate: there is, after all, a limit beyond which taxes cannot be raised (especially since they will never afterwards be reduced again).

Finally, it is possible that Galbraith is making too sharp a distinction between demand-pull and cost-push inflation. The success of corporations in passing on higher wage costs has in the past often been at least partly due to an excessively buoyant level of demand; and thus deflation could conceivably compel the employer to resist the union more intensively or to meet a rise in wages with redundancies (thereby spreading unemployment to the corporate sector as well as the market system). This might be preferable to direct controls if those controls led to evasion, confusion, chaos in production, or to a corporate state where decisions on important issues of stabilisation and social justice were made by a tripartite commission rather than by the people or their elected representatives. Moreover, Galbraith does not specify precise criteria for his Board, except to say that equity and redistribution (and thus average rather than marginal productivity) should substantially influence its decisions on pay. Apart from upsetting traditional differentials and mechanisms, this is a clear recommendation for unequal treatment of equal citizens, which some observers may take as a threat to individual freedom. Nor is it self-evident that controls will be popular: Jack may be poorer than Jill because he is underprivileged, but also because he is lazy, and a policy of redistribution of life-chances via redistribution of income may be a source of considerable resentment (more so, say, than a policy of redistribution of life-chances via an expansion of the welfare state).

In any case, Galbraith assumes that decisions will be tripartite and that the unions will agree to work with the Board. Should they refuse co-operation, however, the ball is returned to the politicians and the bureaucrats, who must both make policy and impose it on an unwilling community. Their powers are increased, but so are their headaches.

28   D. A. REISMAN

Notes and references

All the works cited are by J. K. Galbraith.

1 *Economics and the Public Purpose* (abbreviated in following references to EPP), Penguin 1975, p 164.
2 *The New Industrial State* (abbreviated to NIS), 2nd edn, Penguin 1974, p 61.
3 *A Theory of Price Control*, Harvard University Press 1952, p 66.
4 *EPP*, p 204.
5 *NIS*, chs. 23—4.
6 'Inflation: a Presidential catechism', *New York Times Magazine* 15 September 1974, p 14.
7 *The Affluent Society* (abbreviated to AS), 2nd edn, Penguin 1970, pp 194—5.
8 'Inflation, recession or controls' in *A Contemporary Guide to Economics, Peace and Laughter* (abbreviated to EPL), Penguin 1975, pp 74—5.
9 Consider, for example, the disastrous experience of the postwar boom of 1919 (when the Federal Reserve nonetheless kept interest rates low) and its successor, the deep recession of 1920 (triggered off when the Federal Reserve finally raised its rediscount rate to an unprecedented 6%): 'From mid-1920 on, the United States suffered from what many believe to have been the sharpest depression to that time in its history. The Federal Reserve, facing its first major test, could not be said to have passed with flying or any other colors. By common agreement it assisted the boom and worsened the bust'.
Money: Whence It Came, Where It Went (abbreviated to *Money*), Houghton Miflin 1975, p 169.
10 'Mr Nixon's remedy for inflation', *Harpers Magazine*, February 1960, p 34.
11 'Will the answer be controls?', *The Listener* 30 January 1975, p 130.
12 'Inflation: a Presidential catechism', p 14. In a letter to the author dated 21 August 1975 Galbraith confirms that in practical terms his recommendations do not exclude a measure of flexibility: 'Thus, while I do not like monetary policy and do not believe it a useful and equitable instrument of control, I had difficulty in urging a relaxation of such policy a year ago in the middle of the worst peacetime inflation in our history.'
13 'Mr Nixon's remedy for inflation', p 33.
14 EPP, p 327.
15 NIS, pp 230—1.
16 'Power and the useful economist', *American Economic Review*, March 1973, p 8.
17 *Money*, p 276.
18 'Inflation: a Presidential catechism', p 89.
19 *Ambassador's Journal*, Hamish Hamilton 1969, p 381.
20 'Inflation: a Presidential catechism', p 14.
21 *A China Passage*, Andre Deutsch 1973, p 8.
22 'Inflation: a Presidential catechism', p 87.
23 NIS, p 150.
24 EPP, p 283.

25 AS, p 93.
26 'Perfecting the corporation', *The New Republic* 2 November 1974, p 17.
27 EPP, p 284.
28 'Inflation, recession or controls', p 82.
29 *Money*, pp 273, 278–9.
30 *The American Left and Some British Comparisons*, Fabian Tract 405, 1971, p 31.
31 'Inflation: a Presidential catechism', p 14.
32 'Inflation: what it takes', in *The Liberal Hour*, (abbreviated to LH), Penguin, 1960, p 68.
33 'Will the answer be controls?', p 131.
34 'Inflation, recession or controls', p 80.
35 'Inflation: a Presidential catechism', p 14.
36 'Inflation: what it takes', in LH p 73.
37 'The case for George McGovern', *Saturday Review* 1 July 1972, p 27.
38 EPP, p 278.
39 *Money*, p 293.
40 *Money*, p 304.
41 *Money*, pp 309–310.
42 'Inflation, recession or controls', p 80.
43 *The American Left*, p 32.
44 *A Theory of Price Control*, p 17.
45 'Wage controls: reluctance to accept the inevitable', *The Times* 16 July 1975.
46 *The American Left*, p 31.

MICHAEL JEFFERSON
Head of Economic Environment, Group Planning Division, Shell
International Petroleum Co. Ltd.

3 The concern with inequality in Victorian fiction

Introduction

In recent years there has been renewed interest in Victorian social
fiction, those novels which demonstrate social concern or deal
with social problems whether or not they were didactic in purpose.
This interest has coincided with the development of social history
and literary sociology in higher educational institutions and the
desire to go beyond a few established authors long cherished by
traditional departments of English Literature, sometimes to the
extent of extolling the virtues of the Marxist interpretation of literature. The interest has been reinforced by those masochistic
tendencies evident in the British people during the post-1945
period, which have not gone unrelished elsewhere, derived from
partially true but therefore partially false notions of the nature
and consequences of the industrialisation process; of living and
working conditions in town and factory, village and field, house
and hovel.

The purpose of this paper is to raise questions and indulge in
speculations, of hopefully the useful rather than idle order; not to
reach definitive positions. In particular, the paper concentrates on
the following matters:

How large in volume and variety was Victorian social fiction?
How great an influence has this fiction had on social and political attitudes?

Is there a consistent, or frequent, bias in Victorian social
fiction which may have influenced attitudes in one direction
rather than another?

To what extent was there a concern with inequality in Victorian
social fiction, and has that concern been transmitted down the
generations?

The concern with inequality in Victorian social fiction is here
defined broadly, if not elliptically. It bestrides the concern of the
novelists themselves, of literary critics, of sociologists, of economic
historians, of propagandists and ideologists, and of students.

The Volume and Variety of Victorian Social Fiction

When that excellent introduction to this subject, P. J. Keating's
The Working Classes in Victorian Fiction was published in 1971,
one well-known reviewer wrote: 'A great deal of his material is
altogether new to me . . .' Some of it does, of course, encompass
household names — Charles Dickens, George Eliot, Disraeli,
Mrs Gaskell, Anthony Trollope and Frances Trollope, Mrs Henry
Wood, George Gissing, Thomas Hardy, Rudyard Kipling, Somerset
Maugham and so on. There are, however, perhaps 600 to 700
other Victorian social novels written by long-forgotten authors
which nevertheless enjoyed considerable popularity in their day;
were read to and by a succeeding generation; and which advanced
views, descriptions and precepts which were consciously or unconsciously imbibed and handed down.

The Volume

It is difficult to realise now that G. W. M. Reynolds (and J. F.
Smith) was probably more popular than Dickens in the 1840s, in
a period when *Dombey and Son* and *David Copperfield* were first
published and when even *The Haunted Man* sold 18,000 copies on
the first day. Scanning the shelves of second-hand booksellers one
may occasionally see the initials ALOE, or A Lady of England, but
then she wrote more than 150 works. The most influential novelist from the 1860s to 1880s was probably Mrs C. L. Balfour, not
now a widely known name. Hesba Stretton enjoyed a huge success
with several of her novels, perhaps none bigger than *Jessica's First
Prayer*, which sold over 1½ million copies. Some obviously thought
the novels of M. A. Paull were outstanding, for she wrote two big-
selling Prize Tales for the temperance movement (as Mrs Henry

Wood had done with *Danesbury House* some years before). Edward
Jenkins's *Ginx's Baby* was described in Britain and the United
States as the most popular book in England in 1870, a view reinforced by the novel's 37 editions in the next seven years. W. H.
Mallock wrote a trilogy in the 1890s which excited considerable
political interest and controversy, while Mrs Humphry Ward's
slightly earlier *Robert Elsmere* was at the centre of religious controversy and sold over 70,000 copies in the first three years after
publication. The list is almost endless, but let us close it with three
personal favourites — F. W. Robinson, who wrote over 55 novels,
mainly in the third quarter of the century; Sir Walter Besant, who
co-authored numerous novels with James Rice and then himself
wrote such works as *All Sorts and Conditions of Men, Children
of Gibeon,* and *The Alabaster Box* ; and William Pett Ridge, who
began writing his light and witty yet revealing stories of London
life in the late 1890s and continued until the late 1920s[1].

The Forms

The novels published in parts or serialised in magazines which were
then published in book form, or which were first produced in book
form, do not exhaust the forms Victorian social fiction took. Indeed, there are some who would urge us to look beyond the novels
to street literature, songs and oral story-telling on the grounds that
these were the most popular forms of literature used by the working class; an urging to which we should respond with caution.

   For instance, it is asserted that the traditional novel form was
produced by and for the middle class, and failure to go beyond the
novel form is illustrative of the degree to which we are class-bound[2].
However, even those seeking working-class literature in its purest
form, in Chartist poets and writers for example, fail to make con-
vincing distinctions. W. J. Linton, Ernest Jones, Gerald Massey and
Thomas Cooper are claimed 'to mirror many of the strengths and
difficulties of pioneering a written working-class literature', when
only Massey's background can properly be described as working-
class and he soon left both the class and the radical circles which
lionised him in his early 20s.

   Then there is a tendency among recent writers to seek out little
known examples of such working-class literature, long decaying
on dusty shelves in a few provincial libraries. This activity has
considerable importance and interest in a specialised academic
context, and Martha Vicinus and Ivanka Kovacevic have resurrec-

ted interesting items from obscurity with references in their recent books,[3] as Louis James did a decade earlier[4]. But in many cases works are cited which enjoyed no popular acclaim, are unlikely to have had any significant effect on social or political attitudes, and do not even conform to any revisionist definition of working-class fiction. If we are to seek significant social fiction other than in its book form then the more profitable route is through the popular magazines, the area on which Margaret Dalziel concentrated nearly two decades ago[5]. And if we were to enlarge our understanding of social fiction in book form, then the most profitable route would be through the output of the religious press which R. K. Webb was not alone in drawing attention to before passing on after only a tentative assessment[6].

Nevertheless, it should be recalled — what will be obvious to any frequenter of second-hand bookshops despite the attritions of the pulping industry and export trade — that the social novels were more widely read than even the many large sales figures suggested; not so much through the circulating libraries, frequented by the middle and upper classes, but in the Mechanics' and Artisans' Institutes frequented by the more gifted and industrious working men, who were in the mainstream of the radical and Dissenting tradition and comprised a significant slice of the book-buying public also.

The Variety

The variety of subject tackled in Victorian social fiction is also an impressive feature. It was a genre, after all, which was less numerous than the totality of 'bloods', Gothic novels, Silver Fork romances, and other light fiction published through the century. The early Victorian period is marked by the 'Condition-of-England' novels of the 1840s and early 1850s, concerned with industrial conditions, urban poverty, child labour and brutality; novels concerned with agricultural conditions and others concerned with City financiers and speculative enterprises, both subjects which formed a persistent theme from the 1840s to the end of the century; the temperance novels which blossomed from the late 1850s; and the novels which may still seem to wallow in decadence, brutality and drunkenness that were less frequent in the 1860s and 1870s than they had been in the two previous decades, and much less frequent than they were to be in the two decades following.

Low life in the East End of London was an intermittent theme until the spring became a fashionable torrent in the 1880s and

1890s. Manchester cellar dwellings; dockyard Liverpool; the back streets of Edinburgh; the coalfields of Durham, Northumberland, Lancashire and Staffordshire, all received varying degrees of coverage. The textile industry in Lancashire, Yorkshire and Derbyshire often called forth harsh comment. Conditions in some prisons and lunatic asylums were exposed; the 'rattening' of non-unionists by trades unionists was attacked; and the workings of the Game Laws, truck system, Poor Law Amendment Act of 1834, and factory legislation were fiercely criticised. Insights were given into the working lives of cotton operatives and agricultural labourers, London costermongers and Fenland cheap-jacks, coal miners and climbing boys.

The Influence of Victorian Social Fiction

Given the sheer volume and variety of this social fiction, the fact that quite minor examples were standard occupants of bookshelves in the homes of many working people, the memories of those born earlier this century in humble circumstances with examples of such fiction on their fathers' shelves, it is hardly surprising that its influence has been profound if unmeasurable.

Some years ago a questionnaire was sent to 450 people, care being taken not to include too many people who were thought particularly likely to be influenced by books. A significant number of the respondents were interested in reading of 'an alternative lifestyle', like the respondent who declared that historical novels had altered his attitude 'to life and morals by enlarging my knowledge of life as experienced by people in other societies'. An ex-Chancellor of the Exchequer said that while reading Dickens had not changed his outlook, 'the portrayal of the hardship of the poor under early nineteenth century conditions stimulated my social conscience'. A crane-driver said that *Oliver Twist* had given him a better understanding of the society in which he lived, and that it made him understand the kind of life his grandparents' generation had led. One can imagine some Victorian readers being struck by contemporary fiction as one respondent was by George Orwell's *Down and Out in Paris and London* (especially as these novels not infrequently claimed to be virtually non-fiction, being written 'without exaggeration'), who said his attitude to politics was changed by making him see 'abolishing unemployment and poverty as the most important political and social reforms'. Diana Spear-

man, who conducted the survey, concluded that 'the answers did
not provide any information about the potentially harmful effects
of certain books' despite her recognition that fiction still exercised
a social influence, reinforced views already held or communicated
by press or television, and provided information which although
available from other sources was more compelling in its fictional
form.

In recognising these influential characteristics of fiction Mrs
Spearman implied, perhaps unconsciously, that her conclusion
was too agnostic. It has become generally accepted that literature
may reflect society; it may influence or shape society; and it may
confirm or strengthen cultural norms, attitudes and beliefs[8]. None
of these views can be accepted simplistically or substantiated
readily; however there is a need for a clearer view on this subject
in a context long ago highlighted by Humphry House:

> Dickens is quoted often as indicating the trend of opinion and taste, but
> also on matters of fact, not merely because his familiar words will give
> extra point to an illustration from another source, but because his words
> are so often the best illustration to be had. And as history filters down
> from original researchers and creative historians through the various
> strata of text-books, references to Dickens become more frequent (one
> might add more careless), and of proportionately greater importance.
> The extreme is reached in one of the most popular History Text-Books
> for children between the ages of 11 and 14 . . .[9].

The recent resurgence of interest in social fiction, and the
extent to which it has become required reading in departments
of literature and social history in the United States and — more
recently — in Britain, suggests that these dangers have not diminished. Nor are they confined to these two countries. In a revealing
passage, Professor Kovacevic of the Department of Philology in
the University of Belgrade has recently indicated the interest that
exists in gaining the attention of students in the developing
nations to fiction dealing with the industrialisation process in
Britain:

> In an attempt to meet the needs of the general student as well as the
> specialist, I have also reproduced two or three texts that will be familiar
> to English readers, perhaps, but not to readers on the Continent or in
> more distant parts of the globe. And since the process of industrialization
> will be in its early stages in some of these parts, these accounts of the
> early stages in England may be felt as more directly relevant than they
> can possibly be in Western Europe[10].

In the time and space available to us, the extent and nature of

the influence which Victorian social fiction has had and continues
to have can only be lightly sketched, and given its speculative and
sometimes obvious nature there is no great value in prolonging
the citation of examples and quotations. More interesting is the
reaction which academics and others with a direct, if unperceived,
interest have to this fiction.

Attitudes to Victorian Social Fiction

Professional economic historians have largely ignored social fiction
in their published work. An article by W. O. Aydelotte 'The England of Marx and Mill as reflected in fiction', which appeared in a
Supplement to *The Journal of Economic History* in 1948, is
frequently noted and largely noteworthy because it is an almost
unique example of such a study in the professional literature. An
essay on 'Industrialisation and poverty: in fact and fiction',
published in *The Long Debate on Poverty* in 1972 (2nd edn 1974)
was written by a professional economist, not a professional economic historian. It is characteristic that a book on *The Captain of
Industry in English Fiction, 1821-1841* was written by an Assistant
Professor of English at the University of New Mexico — Ivan
Melada — though he did have some experience of the shipbuilding
industry. References to particular social novels are also extremely
rare in the more specialist works. One thinks of such rare exceptions as Mrs Trollope's *Michael Armstrong,* mentioned by S. D.
Chapman in *The Early Factory Masters,* 1967 and by A. E. Musson
in his article on 'Robert Blincoe and the early factory system'
published first in Derbyshire Miscellany for February 1958 and
reprinted in a revised version in his *Trade Union and Social History*
in 1974.

A more typical attitude is that of Duncan Bythell, who appears
to regard the factual unreliability of social novels as having been
self-evident for decades to all 'outside a few university departments
of English Literature', and not worth pointing out[11]. A variant on
this professional view has been expressed by Asa Briggs in a review
article in *The Financial Times,* early in 1973. Claiming that nobody
seriously believes that the 'Condition of England' novels of the
1840s and 1850s are an accurate representation of the economic
and social facts of their times, and pointing out that they were
sometimes written as a direct attack on statistical evidence, Professor Briggs nevertheless concludes that the novels give an accurate

portrayal of attitudes current at the time (a view to which the
otherwise cautionary Aydelotte was also inclined).

This thesis is open to the following qualifications. First, there
are many people who do believe that such novels give a broadly
accurate representation of the economic and social facts of their
times. Second, the use made of these novels in teaching establish-
ments suggests that the intention goes beyond an attempt to
portray attitudes current at the time. Third, the novels may
provide an accurate portrayal of these attitudes, but this is hardly
to say that they were representative of anything but a small
minority. And where the novelist is trying to capture the attitudes
of fictional characters rather than those of the author, one thinks
of the passage in *Mary Barton* where John Barton has been com-
plaining that the poor alone suffer in bad times, the reader is apt
to forget the author's intention under the weight of her stark
portrayal of immiseration. Mrs Gaskell's plea: 'I know that this is
not really the case; and I know what is the truth in such matters;
but what I wish to impress is what the workman feels and thinks',
falls rather flat. But fourth, and perhaps most important, it is easy
enough for those who believe the early Victorian social novel is an
accurate guide to attitudes, but not to economic or social facts,
to fall into circular reasoning at this point. If the problem is to
determine how accurate a guide to social and economic history
the social novels are, and it is established that the views and interpretations of events expressed do accurately reflect the attitudes
of the time, it does not follow that the novels are a useful guide.
All that follows is that attitudes at the time were not soundly
based on the facts, precisely the problem that has to be explained.

The attitudes of other academics are perhaps more readily understandable. Academic economists, for example, not infrequently
regard economic history as only a little above economic geography
and sociology in their scale of values. A few economists have expressed concern at the suspicion which most intellectuals seem to
have of the market system from the deft touches of George Stig-
ler's *The Intellectual and the Market Place* to the more pungent
criticisms of Arthur Shenfield in such articles as 'The ugly
intellectual' and 'The roots of American discontent'. On the whole,
however, despite their description of atomistic competition as
'Perfect' and any other form as 'Imperfect', academic economists
increasingly tend to view competition as inherently wasteful and
only private monopoly as unacceptable. They are not particularly
sensitive as to why intellectuals might suspect market mechanisms,

and be antipathetic to industry and commerce.

Does Victorian Social Fiction Matter?

But perhaps the most important question to be faced is: Does all
this matter? What is the nature of the errors which may be perpe-
trated by the reading and study of social fiction? Is there a
consistent or frequent bias and, if so, what are its effects?

It matters a great deal that specialists in one academic field
stand aside and observe the misuse and misunderstanding of
material by specialists in another academic discipline. It matters a
great deal if ideological bias is denied or ignored in public controversy. But let us consider one unfamiliar reason why it may matter.

In seeking explanations for Britain's poor economic performance relative to most other advanced industrial nations in recent
years, the widespread antipathy to business, a lack of self-confidence in management, and the attitudes within the trades union
movement, it may not be too fanciful to indict the influence of
social fiction among a multiplicity of relevant factors. A large
strand of the English literary tradition is, after all, arguably
hostile to industrial and commercial enterprise.

In 1825 the bookseller J. S. Gregson remarked on the want of
taste for literature in Manchester, the bulk of the inhabitants
seeming to have such a desire to acquire wealth that anything
superfluous to this end was deemed worthless. He concluded
that 'this insatiable passion for gain cannot co-exist with a love of
literature'.[12] Whatever the explanation, an indifference to literature and even to history — those twin sisters as G. M. Trevelyan
once called them[13] — seems to have been a characteristic of most
businessmen from that day to this.

Of course, it is of the nature of things that businessmen are
close to the economic firing line, intent upon reacting to changes
in markets and output, in prices and costs. Some among them are
deputed to consider future planning and policy, taking a longer-
term view of their activities. But backward glances, save for post-
mortems on the recent past of business success or failure, seem
irrelevant to them. When business enterprise and the businessman
are under external attack the businessman has no weapon of
defence readily to hand except his own experience and a strong
feeling that by his endeavours he is improving the material well-
being of mankind. Yet many of these attacks are founded upon

events in the distant past, or upon misunderstandings about the past based on atypical or transient features, or upon subsequent erroneous — because ideologically biased — interpretations of the past.

The businessman is unable, on the basis of his experience and endeavours, to rebut these attacks in their entirety. Those outside business persist in their belief that the industrial system and commercial practice have a sordid past and remain sordid, if to a less marked degree. Those within business either accept that the past was sordid or confess that they have no means of judging one way or the other. Their self-confidence is reduced and they may even begin to lose confidence that their own business enterprise serves a useful purpose.

A relevant factor here is the clear ideological intent of a growing body of literary criticism and even of fiction itself. Saul Bellow complained some years ago that we no longer have a literary situation but 'a sociological, a political, a psychological situation in which there are literary elements'. An anti-capitalist culture had established itself within the old tradition, with fatal consequences for literature[14]. It is no accident that in what is now a substantial body of articles and books with such titles as 'Literature and Ideology' and 'Literature and Sociology' the names of Russian and East European authors frequently crop up. Their viewpoint may conveniently be illustrated by the words of Professor G. N. Pospelov of the Lomonosov National University of Moscow:

> All creative artists, especially writers and poets, strive to express their emotional interpretation of life in graphic and expressive images in their works because it is their ideological interpretation of life, imbued with emotion and 'pathos'. It is the latter which spurs them to create. The artist's abstract convictions, his ideological views, can also play a more or less important part in stimulating his creative activity[15].

One is inclined to suspect that the major division of opinion within this group of literary sociologists lies between those who concentrate solely on authors with little creative imagination who content themselves with relating experiences of misery while transposing them as little as possible, and those who speculate upon — where they cannot forcibly extract — the ideological undertones of the most gifted and imaginative authors[16]. Almost everything else, including the brighter aspects of life, growing prosperity more generally, and alternative ideologies are ignored or given only fleeting attention. Diana Spearman, in her book *The Novel and Society*, was driven to the view that 'from the political aspect of Marxism one might think that the literature of one age, unless it was a literature of protest, could have no value or interest in another' and charged some Marxist critics with assuming that 'unless an author can somehow be twisted into an exponent of social wrongs, his work is worthless'[17].

Nevertheless, there is nothing reprehensible in judging literary works from an ideological standpoint despite the irritation this causes among traditionalists who believe literature is simply to be enjoyed. George Watson, for instance, reacting to an attempt by Raymond Williams in 1971 to introduce a new Paper into the Cambridge English Tripos entitled 'Literature and Marxism', wrote off Marxist literary interpretation as 'a nineteenth-century dinosaur'. Given some of the absurd claims made by Marxist critics and writers this irritation is understandable. Ralph Fox was neither the first nor the last to claim that 'a Socialist art, a new realism, is to-day alone capable of that complete objectivity which permits the creative worker to win in his ardent battle with reality'[18]. The danger lies in the naivete of those who fail to recognise the ideological undertones and intent, and who ignore the perversity or sinister aims of those who deny the ideological content and deride contrary views — those who see no significance, for example, in the fact that a novel by Charles Reade: *Put Yourself In His Place,* which deals with attacks on non-unionists by trades unionists and is rather well-written and significant, is widely ignored nowadays in favour of lesser works which attack the capitalist system rather than the labour movement.

One must be careful, however, not to go to the other extreme. Ludwig von Mises assumed that 'social' and 'socialist' novels and plays were synonymous[19]. This is to go altogether too far. There are many sympathetic studies of businessmen in Victorian social fiction; there were few outright expressions of sympathy with Chartism, as novelists shrank from advocating or sympathising with violence; some novelists were advocates of self-help, hesitant about meeting the full aspirations of militant working men and recognising that fecklessness was one avoidable cause of poverty; later in the century many of the novelists writing about the slums of London's East End were more concerned with the monotony of living conditions than with absolute poverty, more aware of the brutality of human beings than of the imperfections of an economic system.

Recognising the limitations of many generalisations in this field, there are nevertheless some general statements that can be made with confidence. The novelist inevitably personalises and caricatures issues and events through the experiences of fictional characters, which makes them more compelling, and by the act of publication also suggests they have a generalised significance and truth. Many, but not all, novelists concerned with industrial or urban poverty tended to portray the worst examples in the worst places, sometimes because they relied on Blue Book evidence which itself was often based on the atypical case[20].

This tendency was sometimes disguised by the novelists themselves. Mrs Trollope in *Michael Armstrong* challenged her readers: 'Let none dare to say this picture is exaggerated, till he has taken the trouble to ascertain by his own personal investigation that it is so . . .'. Mrs Tonna in *Helen Fleetwood* was even firmer: 'Let no one suppose we are going to write fiction . . . we will set forth nothing but what has been stated on oath, corroborated on oath, and on oath confirmed beyond the possibility of an evasive question'. In this context it is interesting to cite a somewhat improbable source, A. H. N. Green-Armytage writing in *The Downside Review*, 1972 on 'The truth of fiction'. Announcing that he could not claim to be an expert on either fiction or truth, the author stated that as regards truth:

> If I cannot make that claim myself it is certain that the novelists can and do. They all assert that truth is their stock-in-trade.

He goes on to quote Nathaniel Hawthorne, Joseph Conrad, Thackeray, Dostoevsky and Zola in support[21].

The novelist's viewpoint is normally a cross-sectional one of a particular place at a particular time or narrow period, and it is difficult to analyse and portray change and progress. Novels set in Manchester or Liverpool in the 1840s did not stress how atypical conditions were, how gravely they had been affected by Irish immigration, or what living conditions were like in the suburbs and surrounding areas. Sir James Kay-Shuttleworth, William Cooke Taylor, Charles Turner Thackrah, W. R. Greg and many others stressed this point in non-fictional writings but it did not permeate the novels. It was rare for novelists to get the past into perspective, and in the 1840s there was a positive fashion for mediaevalism and a belief in a past Golden Age. The impact of the Napoleonic Wars was rarely recognised, although historical social novels such as Charlotte Bronte's *Shirley*, Mrs Craik's *John Halifax, Gentleman*, and Mrs Linnaeus Banks's *The Manchester Man* were noteworthy exceptions. Instead there was a tendency to assert a decline in the general standard of living in the early part of the century without firm evidence or ascertaining a cause external to the economic system, Charles Kingsley's *Yeast* and Mrs Gaskell's *Mary Barton* and *Ruth* providing good examples of this trait. Indeed, one is inclined to believe that only Charles Dickens of the social novelists of the time turned his back firmly on a past Golden Age and looked with some enthusiasm to the future. There were also cases where authors wrote historical fiction as if it were a current analysis, such as Mrs Trollope's *Michael Armstrong*. This novel was apparently set in the late 1830s although in reality it relied upon a suspect source dealing with the years 1806-1807. This was not an isolated instance, but legislative and other changes made this novel a particularly misleading source of information despite its availability in two modern hard-bound reprints.

The social novelists, on the whole, shared a suspicion of classical economists and the competitive system. They thought little, as Charles Kingsley put it in *Alton Locke*, of 'the calculations of the great King Laissez-faire' which were likely to prove — as Charles Dickens remarked in *Hard Times* — that 'the Good Samaritan was a Bad Economist'. Only Mrs Gaskell, in the Preface to *Mary Barton*, confessed ignorance of Political Economy, the rest attacked what they conceived it to be.

But then the social novelists were more concerned with the description of effects than with the analysis of causes — compelling descriptions of poverty, inequality, brutality and drunkenness: not much on the mutual advantage implied by a bargain being struck; on what the classical economists actually thought and wrote; or on the benefits of competition in lowering prices, defeating monopoly, encouraging progress and undermining bastions of privilege. Nor were their readers necessarily more critical. Mrs Cooke Taylor, fresh from a tour of industrial Lancashire, noted the following experience in a London drawing room in 1843. An apparently clever and intelligent man was discoursing on the starved, oppressed and overworked people as contrasted with the bloated and pampered race of mill-owners. Challenged as to where he had seen such misery, he replied that he never had seen it but had been told it existed. Mrs Cooke Taylor expressed irritation at those 'who spread reports without even taking the trouble of inquiring if they be true or false'[22].

To the question: is there a consistent or frequent bias in Victorian social fiction? the answer must be negative on consistency but positive on frequency — sufficiently frequent, we suggest,

to amount to that tradition of hostility to industrial and
commerical activity which has often been remarked upon,
manifestations of an economic system which was widely blamed
for the inequality which existed.

The Concern With Inequality

The social novelists were not merely concerned with particular
economic systems, of course, but many did focus on the inequalities which either they felt the system gave rise to or which (as in
the case of Mrs Gaskell mentioned earlier) people felt, whether or
not they correctly discerned the cause.

    The recognition of inequality took many forms. It might be
done obviously, as indicated by the title of Douglas Jerrold's
St Giles and St James which compared and contrasted the poverty
of the former with the luxury of the latter. This novel had certain
parallels with Sir Walter Besant's much later *Children of Gibeon*.
There is Edward Jenkins's *Ginx's Baby* as compared with his *Lord
Bantam*. Or, more subtly, there is the contrast of life styles where
the only real connecting link might be the disease which could
readily pass from the hovel to the visiting rich, as in Charles
Kingsley's *Yeast,* and from the dying tailor to the rich customer
as in *Alton Locke.* The out-of-work cotton operative might gnash
his teeth at his ex-employer's family stepping into a coach laden
with their purchases. The starving, agitating for food and justice,
feel the deep injustice of being cut down by the Yeomanry. Sexual
inequality is also a frequent theme, but mainly indirectly through
the plight of brutalised and 'fallen' women from Mrs Trollope's
Jessie Phillips and various Dickens' characters to Thomas Hardy
and other writers towards the end of the century. There are few
which deal with sexual inequality in more positive terms. One has
to look, much later in the century, at George Gissing's *The
Emancipated* (1890) and *The Odd Women* (1893), Thomas
Hardy's *Jude the Obscure* (1895), and Grant Allen's *The Woman
Who Did* (1895) for the non-traditional appreciations. Towards
the end of the century social inequality became an old theme
with a difference. The heroine gives away her money for a People's
Palace in Besant's *All Sorts and Conditions of Men*; a son atones
for his father's property-dealings in the East End by working
among the poor in Besant's *The Alabaster Box*; loss of a fortune
and the opening of a grocery shop is not a disaster for Gissing's

Will Warburton; and a clergyman gives up a comfortable living to work in London's East End, in Mrs Humphry Ward's *Robert Elsmere*.

Yet there is curious difficulty after reading Victorian social fiction and literary sociology in grasping the material advancement, social mobility, and reduction in inequality which took place during this period or the causes of these changes. It is curious because there are novels about self-made men; about the virtues of hard work, temperance and thrift in achieving advancement and prosperity; and one or two about the sea-change which appeared to take place in material standards of living in the early 1850s.

The evidence for this progress, where not conceded as self-evident, is beyond the scope of this paper, but one small example may usefully be given — social mobility in Lancashire, where it is often supposed that the social mobility indicated in the 'Condition of England' novels, *Mary Barton, North and South, Sybil,* and *Hard Times,* for example, was a mere flash in the pan. A survey conducted in the Lancashire cotton industry just before the First World War showed that of a random sample of cotton manufacturers 76% of the respondents (there was a 70% response to the survey) were employers of the first generation, who had begun their working lives as operatives or clerks without family connections or financial backing[23].

Conclusion

The point to be driven home is that if we are to use social fiction as historical documentation, whether we are economists or economic historians or social historians or literary sociologists or just plain students of English Literature, then we must be extremely cautious in that use. The time has passed when the professional economic historian could patronisingly smirk at the literary sociologist getting his history wrong, and pass by on the other side. The time has passed when academic disciplines could exist side by side and not communicate. There is a need for more interdisciplinary studies, not as a soft option but as a necessary corrective to ideological bias and just plain ignorance. Despite the growth and findings of modern social history in recent years, these problems remain with us and may have been exacerbated.

Let me end by reminding you how prevalent and significant the issues we have been dealing with here are. Not long ago an anonymous reviewer in *The Times Literary Supplement* took no less a person than Professor Dorothy Marshall to task:

> In the nineteenth century her acceptance of novels as sources of information is often surprising. Surely no one could now consider Mrs Gaskell's books — interesting though they are as documents of their period — to be reliable sources of information about the lives of the working people, still less about their thoughts or their political activities. Still less are the works of Kingsley and Disraeli in intention or effect sources to be taken with any but the most careful counter-checking. Yet these are the voices heard most often in the infrequent quotations, with the exception of that of Edwin Chadwick[24].

Anybody familiar with the curricula and set-readings of some of our universities and secondary educational institutions will recognise how excessively optimistic the reviewer's viewpoint is. And to anyone interested in the level and quality of academic debate and public controversy, in the transmission of sound rather than unsound ideas to the young, or in attitudes towards industry and commerce, the causes and incidence of poverty, and the British economy in general, this should be a matter of deep concern worthy of closer study.

Notes and references

1 The author arranged an exhibition of Victorian social fiction in the library of the University of Surrey to coincide with the meeting of the British Association for the Advancement of Science. An exhibition catalogue and list of other significant titles was compiled and introduced by Michael Jefferson and is available from The National Book League, London.

2 Martha Vicinus provides a recent instance in *The Industrial Muse*, Croom Helm 1974.

3 Ivanka Kovacevic, *Fact into Fiction: English Literature and the Industrial Scene, 1750-1850*, Leicester University Press 1975.

4 Louis James, *Fiction for the Working Man, 1830-1850*, Oxford University Press 1963.

5 Margaret Dalziel, *Popular Fiction 100 Years Ago: An Unexplored Tract of Literary History*, Cohen & West 1957.

6 R. K. Webb, *The British Working Class Reader, 1790-1848: Literacy and Social Tension*, Allen & Unwin 1955, p 25.

7 Diana Spearman, 'The social influence of fiction', *New Society* 6 July 1972.

8 Milton C. Albrecht, 'The relationship of literature and society', *American Journal of Sociology*, vol. 59, 1954, pp 425-436.

9 Humphry House, *The Dickens World*, Oxford University Press 1942, p 9.

10 Ivanka Kovacevic, 1975, p 16.

11 Duncan Bythell, 'The history of the poor: a review article', *The English Historical Review*, April 1974, p 370.

12 Quoted in H. J. Dyos and M. Wolff, *The Victorian City: Images and Realities*, Routledge & Kegan Paul 1973, p 740.

13 G. M. Trevelyan, *History and the Reader*, Cambridge University Press 1945, p 14.

14 Saul Bellow, 'Culture now', *Modern Occasions*, Winter 1971.

15 G. N. Pospelov, 'Literature and sociology', *International Social Science Journal*, vol. XIX, no. 4, 1967, pp 542-543.

16 Lucien Goldmann, 'The sociology of literature: status and problems of method', *International Social Science Journal*, vol. XIX, no. 4, 1967 pp 494-495.

17 Diana Spearman, *The Novel and Society*, Routledge & Kegan Paul 1966, p 3.

18 Ralph Fox, *The Novel and The People*, Cobbett Press 1944, p 41.

19 Ludwig von Mises, *The Anti-Capitalistic Mentality*, Libertarian Press 1956, p 66.

20 Not that the novelists followed the Blue Books with accuracy even where their reliance was greatest; indeed, it was sometimes considered that Blue Books and fiction were indistinguishable. See: Patrick Brantlinger, 'Blue Books, the social organism, and the Victorian novel', *Criticism*, vol XIV, no. 4, 1972, pp 328-344.

Sheila M. Smith, 'Propaganda and hard facts in Charles Reade's didactic novels: a study of *It Is Never Too Late To Mend* and *Hard Cash*', *Renaissance and Modern Studies*, IV, 1960, pp 135-149.

Sheila M. Smith, 'Willenhall and Wodgate: Disraeli's use of Blue Book evidence', *Review of English Studies*, vol. 13, 1962, pp 368-384.

W. H. Chaloner, 'Mrs Trollope and the early factory system', *Victorian Studies*, vol. IX, no. 2, December 1960

21 A. H. N. Green-Armytage, 'The truth of fiction', *The Downside Review*, 1972, p 90.

22 Quoted in F. A. Hayek, *Capitalism and the Historians*, Routledge & Kegan Paul 1954, p 20.

23 S. J. Chapman and E. J. Marquis, 'The recruiting of the employing classes from the ranks of the wage-earners in the cotton industry', *Journal of the Royal Statistical Society*, vol. LXXV, part III, February 1912.

24 *The Times Literary Supplement* (22 June 1973) reviewing *Industrial England 1776-1851*.

T. W. HUTCHISON
Professor of Economics, University of Birmingham

4 Economists and social justice in the history of economic thought

I assume that the subject set before me is not so much one of economists' general ideas and conceptions about the nature of social justice, but is concerned more specifically with the doctrines of economists, at different periods in the history of the subject, regarding how economic policies, institutions and arrangements promote, diminish, or affect social justice in one sense or another; or of how economists have held social justice to be related to the objectives of economic policy.

Questions of the social justice of economic policies and institutions could be regarded primarily as questions of the distribution of income and wealth. How much each person ultimately gets, in real terms after taxes and subsidies or transfers, as compared with everyone else, could be regarded as the ultimate economic outcome of a politico-economic system, and of its policies and institutions, by which, primarily, its justice is to be appraised. But, of course, social justice may be regarded as depending not simply on how much each person gets as compared with other people, but also on how, or on what terms, he or she gets it. In fact, the distribution of incomes and wealth, together with social justice, is affected not simply by the policy instruments of taxes, transfers, and pricing, which bear directly on distribution, but by the whole range of economic policies and institutional arrangements. However, I cannot, of course, cover in this very limited historical survey the doctrines of economists regarding the effects and

47

workings, in terms of social justice, of the whole range of
economic policies. I shall focus primarily on the treatment of
distribution, or re-distribution, via taxation, transfers, and subsidies; but also, when touching upon the more recent or contemporary phases, I shall discuss briefly the attitudes of British
economists in two other areas of economic policy which are
especially critical in terms of social justice in 1975: these are,
first, employment policy and the questions of justice involved in
the incidence of unemployment, or in what has been called 'the
right to work'; and second, questions of stability of the currency
and the incidence of inflation, which may now be seen as a cause
of social injustice to an extent unprecedented in this country in
peace time.

        The earliest European thinking about political
economy and economics was rooted in a predominantly normative
system of ethical and political philosophy in which economic
problems had mostly a very subordinate role. However, just as
there are, or may be, normative elements in what purports to be,
or in what is predominantly, a body of positive theory or analysis,
so, in what was predominantly a normative framework, there could
be found positive implications, or predictions, about the effects of
different institutional arrangements or policies. So it was with the
analysis, by Greek and Medieval philosophers, of economic justice
in prices and in borrowing and lending. As de Roover and Schum-
peter have shown, what was seen as the just price tended to be the
competitive price or, at any rate, certainly *not* a monopoly price
or one distorted by economic power.

    By the time of the emergence of modern political economy in
the hundred years before *The Wealth of Nations,* explicit concern
with justice had been blurred somewhat by the ambiguities, or the
dual character, of the natural law concepts. As Henry Sidgwick
said regarding the influence of the natural law idea on classical
political economy:

> Political Economy became primarily a study of 'what is' rather than of
> 'what ought to be done'; but this was because the two notions were, at
> least to a considerable extent, identified in the political economists'
> contemplation of the existing processes of the production and distribu-
> tion of wealth . . . Misunderstanding has been a good deal aided by the
> ambiguity of the term 'natural', applied by Adam Smith, Ricardo and

others, to the shares of different producers as determined by the economic
laws which these writers expound. For by the term 'natural' as commonly
used, the notion of 'what generally is' or 'what would be apart from
human interference' is suggested in vague combination with 'what ought
to be' or 'what is intended by a benevolent Providence': and it is not
always easy to say in what proportions the two meanings are mixed by
any particular writer.[1]

Certainly the adjective 'natural' seemed to imply that the
natural price was the 'right' and the just and beneficent price. It
was the application of this adjective to wages and the identification
of the 'natural' wage with, in some versions (especially Ricardo's),
a severely restricted and persistent subsistence wage, which led to
questions regarding the beneficence of the 'natural' price of
labour. This questioning of the term 'natural' led on to a clearer
and more explicit distinction between normative and positive.

Concern with justice was also blurred or submerged not only
by the concepts and terminology of the natural law philosophy,
but also by the utilitarian concepts and formulae (as they still
sometimes are blurred in economic 'welfare' analysis). Questions
of justice could be regarded as settled by calculating maxima, or
optima, in respect of pleasure or welfare. Such formulae were
regarded — by, for example, James Mill, the tutor or mentor of
Ricardo — as providing very certain and clear guidelines for policy-
decisions:

> Legislation is essentially a science the effects of which may be computed
> with an extraordinary degree of certainty; and the friends of human
> nature cannot proceed with too much energy in beating down every
> obstacle which opposes the progress of human welfare . . . The ends are
> there, in the first place, known — they are clear and definite. What you
> have after that to determine is the choice of the means, and under glorious
> helps for directing the judgment.[2]

The ambiguities of the natural law concepts and the utilitarian
formulae were clarified somewhat by the sharper distinction
between positive and normative, and the explicit proclamation of
political economy as an ethically and politically 'neutral' science,
in the essays of Senior and J. S. Mill, both dating from 1836.
Senior explicitly put justice outside the confines of the science of
political economy:

> The questions: to what extent and under what circumstances the possession
> of wealth is, on the whole, beneficial or injurious to its possessor, or to the
> society of which he is a member? what distribution of wealth is most
> desirable in each different state of society? and what are the means by
> which any given country can facilitate such a distribution? — all these are

questions of great interest and difficulty, but no more form part of the
Science of Political Economy, in which we use the term, than navigation
forms part of the Science of Astronomy.[3]

However, Senior's rather austere, self-denying methodological
precepts have often not been accepted or followed by economists,
some of whom have from time to time believed themselves to be
well qualified to pronounce and preach on justice in distribution
as well as many other controversial ethical and political questions.

The English classical economists, on the whole,
believed strongly in the justice of the simple system of natural
liberty, except, of course, where its principles had been contra-
dicted by the encroachment of monopoly or monopsony (which
came to be regarded as the case with land ownership). The classical
beliefs included a belief in the far-reaching sanctity of private
property (somewhat qualified in the case of land) as providing the
essential basis for natural liberty, and to be strictly defended
against the intervention of governments. With regard to taxation
the implication was that the inevitable minimum for defence,
justice, and certain public works, must be levied so as to leave the
'natural' distribution as nearly as possible after taxation as it was
before; and this was usually interpreted as justifying a very low
level of taxation on proportional and not progressive scales. In
more 'positive' terms, the sanctity of private property, except for
very low proportional taxation, was regarded as essential for the
preservation of incentives for work and saving necessary for
economic progress. These principles were regarded by Ricardo,
for example, who held them in a most thorough-going form, as
so obviously in the interests even of the poorest in the community,
that he considered that the franchise could safely be extended to
the poorest without any danger to the then existing distribution
of income and wealth (though he was prepared to deprive of the
franchise any who wished to upset the sanctity of private property):

> The last point for consideration is the supposed disposition of the people
> to interfere with the rights of property. *So essential does it appear to me,*
> *to the cause of good government that the rights of property should be*
> *held sacred, that I would agree to deprive those of the elective franchise*
> *against whom it could justly be alleged that they considered it their*
> *interest to invade them.* But in fact it can only be amongst the most

needy in the community that such an opinion can be entertained. The man of a small income must be aware how little his share would be if all the large fortunes in the kingdom were equally divided among the people. He must know that the little he would obtain by such a division could be no adequate compensation for the overturning of a principle which renders the produce of his industry secure. Whatever might be his gains after such a principle had been admitted would be held by a very insecure tenure, and the chance of his making any future gains would be greatly diminished; for the quantity of employment in the country must depend, not only on the quantity of capital, but upon its advantageous distribution, and, above all, on the conviction of each capitalist that he will be allowed to enjoy unmolested the fruits of his capital, his skill, and his enterprise. To take from him this conviction is at once to annihilate half the productive industry of the country, and would be more fatal to the poor labourer than to the rich capitalist himself. *This is so self-evident, that men very little advanced beyond the very lowest stations in the country cannot be ignorant of it, and it may be doubted whether any large number even of the lowest would, if they could, promote a division of property.* [4]

The overriding priority which Ricardo gave to the sanctity of private property, and its defence against taxation, over the relief of poverty and unemployment was further demonstrated by his attitude to the relief of the distress of the handloom cotton weavers in 1820. A Mr Maxwell MP had proposed that consideration be given to the taxing of power looms and to 'the application of public money to provide lands for those who could obtain no employment at their looms'. Ricardo's opposition was indignant and total:

If government interfered, they would do mischief and no good. They had already interfered, and done mischief by the poor laws. The principles of the hon. mover would likewise violate the sacredness of property, which constituted the great security of society. [5]

In any case, the population and natural wage doctrine, as propagated in its most severe form, again by Ricardo, narrowly limited, or even more or less eliminated, any questions as to how the distribution of income and wealth could be modified by public finance so as to enhance social justice.

The ideas of the classical economists regarding social justice certainly had little or no room for egalitarianism. But extreme inequality was regarded by Ricardo as justified on the Rawlsian principle of its being in the interests of the poorest. It was held that such hopes as there were of alleviating poverty depended on economic progress, the essential means and incentives for which in turn depended on what might be called the most thoroughgoing feasible distributive laissez-faire.

        With J. S. Mill a new beginning can, to a rather
restricted extent, be discerned, of a concern with equity and
justice in distribution and with the possibilities of redistribution.
Mill's concern even in its limited form, was comparatively novel
compared with the laissez-faire distributive dogmas of Ricardo.
But Mill was discussing questions much more of future prospects
and possibilities, still some way over the horizon, than present or
immediate practical propositions and policies. We get, for example,
Mill's well-known distinction between the laws of *production,* as
'physical truths' about which 'there is nothing optional or arbitrary'; and *distribution* which depends on the laws and customs of
society, and which is 'very different in different ages and countries
and might be still more different *if mankind so chose.*'[6]
        But in Mill's view, for the present, mankind did *not* so choose
and 'the existing customs of society', as represented in a pretty
hard-line version of the population and natural wage doctrine, for
the time being at any rate, very much confined the immediate or
shorter-run possibilities for a beneficent amendment, via public
finance, of the 'natural' distribution of incomes and wealth. In any
case, before 1867, there was hardly an electoral base which could
be mobilised on behalf of progressive public finance.
        However, Mill's discussion of justice in taxation does break some
new ground and represents a certain shift from the earlier classical
anti-progressive principle. It is true that Mill was opposed to progression in the income tax, beyond exempting a subsistence minimum, and at one stage referred to progressive income taxation as
'a mild form of robbery'. But he did argue for quite drastic
progression in inheritance or estate duties (which was eventually
the channel by which in 1894 progression was introduced into the
British tax system).

        Questions of distributive justice and of the redistribu-
tion of income and wealth only gradually began again to come into
their own, after the decline and fall of the English classical regime;
that is, after the rather sudden loss of credibility of what Jevons
called 'the Ricardo-Mill economics' was succeeded, for a decade or

so, by the, at first, very slow and gradual build-up of what is now
described as 'neo-classical economics'. Regarding the history of
this transition a 'radical' version has been propagated (which, not
to put too fine a point on it, might be described as the product of
sheer fantasy, undiluted and undisciplined by any concern for
historical fact or evidence) according to which after 1870 laissez-
faire became much more of a rigid, orthodox dogma among
economists than it had been previously among the classicals (even
with Ricardo, who might accurately be described as the leading
British economist of any period who generally came nearest to
propagating crude laissez-faire doctrines *over the major areas of
policy where social justice has been mainly involved, that is,
distribution and employment*).[7]

In fact, it was with the major neo-classicals that laissez-faire
doctrines with regard to distribution and social justice began —
for better or for worse — to be fundamentally superseded. For
example, it was Marshall's mentor, Henry Sidgwick, who in his
Principles (1883) explicitly proclaimed justice in distribution
to be one of the two major objectives of economic policy (though
he was not yet ready for progressive income taxation). Together
with 'making the proportion of produce to population a maximum,' Sidgwick proclaimed as the second objective of economic
policy:

> ... rightly distributing produce among members of the community,
> whether on any principle of Equity or Justice, or on the economic
> principle of making the whole produce as useful as possible.[8]

(Ricardo would have been horrified and might even have demand-
ed the disfranchisement of Sidgwick for threatening the rights of
property.)

Two major developments in economic theory, one negative and
one positive, were mainly responsible for this new 'neo-classical'
concern with distribution and justice (together with the external
factor in promoting the transformation of ideas constituted by
the increased electoral or political power of the less well-off after
the reforms in the franchise of 1867 and 1884).

First, and negatively, there was the loss of credibility, in the
face of mid-Victorian prosperity, of the hard empirical content
still propagated in the natural wage doctrine of 'the Ricardo-Mill
economics' (which had been most severely and consequentially
upheld by Ricardo). This fading away of what J. E. Cairnes
(1874) still called 'the great Malthusian difficulty' opened up

the problem of poverty, and brought it onto the agenda for social and economic reform, from which it had been largely excluded under the classical regime. It led Marshall to proclaim eventually to the Royal Commission on the Aged Poor (1893):

> I have devoted myself for the last 25 years to the problem of poverty, and very little of my work has been devoted to any inquiry which does not bear upon that . . .

Marshall went on regarding the austere poor relief policies, still influenced by Ricardian ideas:

> All these statements about wages are repetitions of doctrines that were universal among the economists of the beginning of the century . . .
> The doctrine is that if you tax the rich and give money to the working classes, the result will be that the working classes will increase in number, and the result will be you will have lowered wages in the next generation; and the grant will not have improved the position of the working classes on the whole. As regards this *a change has come, which separates the economics of this generation from the economics of the past . . . That change insists upon the fact that if the money is so spent as to increase the earning power of the next generation, it may not lower wages.*[9]

In his evidence to the Royal Commission on the Aged Poor Marshall was constantly fighting against the persistent influence, in the current authoritative Poor Law literature, of the Ricardian doctrines — a 'relic of old economics' as he described it — (just as Keynes was to have to fight the Ricardian doctrine against public works, still maintained in the Treasury in 1929):

> Whenever I read Poor Law literature of today I am taken back to the beginning of the century; everything that is said about economics has the flavour of that old time.[10]

The second and positive theoretical innovation introduced, or reintroduced, after 1870 was the bringing back of the utility concept into an explicitly central and fundamental place in economic theorising, from which it had been displaced, for about a century, *not* in the mainstream of European theorising, but in the provincial Anglican value-doctrine of the English classicals. From the diminishing utility principle implications were now drawn, notably by Edgeworth, which purported, validly or invalidly, to justify very drastic progression in taxation, just at the moment when powerful electoral forces were beginning to move the British taxation system towards progression in the 1890s. Though he did not irresponsibly shrug off the possible effects of progressive taxation on the supply of effort and saving, Marshall went along with increasing progression in taxation during his later years, accepting, for example, the Lloyd George Budget of 1909 as 'a Social Welfare Budget.'[11]

We are not concerned here with the validity or invalidity of the argument for progressive taxation derived from the diminishing utility proposition. This argument later came under fundamental criticism. We are only concerned with the political intention, or direction of 'neo-classical' arguments, notably those of Edgeworth, to whom Professor Hayek attributes the major intellectual influence in the emergence of progression in this country.[12] The opinion is worth quoting of Dr. Shehab's scholarly historical monograph on progressive taxation:

> The development of this progressive distributional theory at the close of the last century and the beginning of the present one is particularly instructive. Whether we accept it in the form Edgeworth developed, with social utility as its ultimate end, or that of Cannan which attempts to associate welfare with equity, and interprets the latter in terms of the former, or in Professor Pigou's synthesis, we arrive at the same goal; namely the higher taxation of the rich in order to ameliorate the inequality of income distribution, and to procure optimum welfare. This end, it will be observed, is the same ultimate objective at which Socialists aim. Thus, for the first time, and after a whole century of laissez-faire, which the economists professed completely to support, the coalescence between academic discussion of tax distribution and popular demands was accomplished, a coalescence which the prominence of laissez-faire in English economic thought previously made inconceivable.[13]

Regarding the neo-classical marginal productivity analysis of the pricing of the factors of production, very few economists seem to have regarded it as possessing anything like the same rigid restrictive force claimed for the Ricardian 'laws', or indeed, as possessing much content at all. One or two passages from J. B. Clark in the nineties are somewhat monotonously quoted and requoted to the effect that in competitive markets the pricing of the factors of production represents a kind of justice. But what Clark said about the prevalence of monopoly is left carefully unquoted:

> The industrial system which developed under a regime of freedom and competition has become perverted by the presence of monopoly . . .
> *I know of no more startling and disquieting tendency of recent times than the growth of those great corporations which have gathered themselves, each in its own field, nearly all the business that is there transacted.*[14]

Indeed far from regarding it as justifying the existing distribution of income and wealth, Marshall held that the marginal productivity analysis was not a theory at all,[15] while Edgeworth interpreted it in the most modest and cautious terms as consisting of hints and metaphors and warnings. Edgeworth expressly rejected the view that competition 'affords the ideal condition for the distribution of wealth' when the labourer 'gets his product':

> The coincidence of perfect competition with ideal justice is by no means evident to the impartial spectator: much less is it likely to be accepted by the majority of those concerned, whose views must be taken into account by those who would form a theory that has some relation to the facts. One who has closely observed popular movements in America testifies to 'the growing belief that mechanical science and invention applied to industry are too closely held by private enterprise.[16]

The conceptual and theoretical changes which marked the transition ('revolutionary' or otherwise) from the classical Ricardo–Mill doctrines to 'neo-classical' economics, not only gradually opened up the major issues of poverty, distribution, and progressive taxation, which had been mainly closed under the classical regime. The concern with poverty led in the eighties and nineties to a new concern with unemployment as a major cause of poverty. The problem of unemployment had also been closed off and hardly taken seriously, by the classicals, except Malthus, not even by J. S. Mill. 'Irregularities of employment', as Foxwell called them, were seen as a major cause of poverty, and public relief works were proposed, not so much as a means of macroeconomic management, but primarily to relieve poverty. Chamberlain's Circular of 1886, approved in *The Times* by Marshall, though of little quantitative importance, was of considerable intellectual significance, and would, of course, have been dogmatically denounced by Ricardo, the great pioneer of what later came to be called 'the Treasury view', who had strongly protested in Parliament against similar public works proposals in the depression of 1819.

By the end of the 19th century it was coming to be realised that the economic system (with its existing monetary framework) was not so beneficently or even optimally self-adjusting, in terms of the aggregate level of employment as the 'classical' writers had mostly suggested, and that 'crises', cycles, and aggregate fluctuations brought a serious amount of unemployment, which was not to be dismissed in the facile manner of Ricardo and J. S. Mill. In fact a transformation of attitudes was coming about as to social justice in relation to employment and unemployment, and regarding the responsibility resting on the individual worker for finding himself employment, which was assumed to be fully available under classical and Ricardian assumptions. By 1884 Marshall was insisting as against the dogmas emanating from Ricardian economics that:

> Being without the means of livelihood must be treated not as a crime, but as a cause for uncompromising inspection and inquiry.[17]

As José Harris has observed in her distinguished and scholarly work regarding subsequent developments:

> The formation of new Liberal ideas on unemployment policy was merely an aspect of a much wider revolution in the Liberal attitude to social administration which occurred during the 1900s . . . Theoretically it was made possible by certain shifts of emphasis in orthodox economics, particularly the teaching of Alfred Marshall that gratuitous payments to persons in need did not necessarily depress wages, nor discourage thrift, nor act as an incentive to reckless procreation . . . This new teaching was a necessary prelude to the adoption of more positive attitudes towards social distress, and the abandonment of a policy based on 'deterrence'; and it was reflected in the writings of many of the new generation of enthusiasts for social reform.[18]

By 1908 Pigou, in his inaugural lecture on succeeding Marshall, was explicitly denouncing the Ricardian dogma against public works, the first time that had been done by a major, 'orthodox' English economist (apart from Malthus), while in the following year proposals for counter-cyclical public works were being put forward by the Webbs in the Minority Report of the Royal Commission on the Poor Law. In fact, according to José Harris opinion had so advanced that

> by 1914 fatalistic acceptance of the inevitability of the trade cycle and doctrinaire prejudice against the relief of unemployment seemed to have largely passed away.[19]

Plainly there is much truth in this generalisation. Although the Ricardian dogmas were to make something of a come-back in the Treasury in 1929, a fundamental shift in most economists' attitudes regarding the injustice of unemployment had taken place.

For the twenty *peace-time* years between 1914 and
1944, when the White Paper on Employment Policy was published,
the most obvious and overwhelming economic source of social
injustice was unemployment. In these years, right down to the
beginning of the Second World War attitudes regarding unemployment continued to develop along the course on which they had
been launched between 1886 and 1914. More broadly, developments in economic ideas, on the one hand, and in conceptions of
social justice, on the other, were to lead on, via the upheavals of
two world wars, to the welfare state and the mixed economy. But
in economics the inter-war years were those of what has been
called 'High Theory' (whatever, exactly, the adjective, and perhaps
the noun also, denote in this context). Certainly there were
volumes of rather vacuous conceptual and geometrical elaboration,
blended with dogmatic and ambiguous pronouncements, generating
prolonged controversies, about what 'determines' or 'governs'
what. According to Professor Patinkin[20], the development of
Keynes's theorising may be seen as 'The Saga of Man's Struggle
for Freedom from the Quantity Theory' — a freedom of which
many economists, thirty years after the Liberator's death, seem by
no means eager to avail themselves. But as regards *policies,* when
Keynes turned to the unemployment problem in 1924, he started
from where his instigator, Lloyd George, and the leading pre-war
thinkers, had left off ten years previously. Furthermore, as Sir Roy
Harrod has observed, the kind of policies against unemployment
advocated by Keynes from 1924 onwards, changed very little,
apart from some shifts of emphasis, throughout all the intense
intellectual struggle for 'Freedom from the Quantity Theory',
over the next decade or so. Also, incidentally, these policies were
always (except regarding the return to gold) in close agreement
with those advocated by the arch-'classical' A. C. Pigou, between
whom and Keynes, on policy issues, there was, as Keynes himself
put it, 'really *extremely little*'.[21]

With the proclamation in 1944 of a high and stable
level of employment as an agreed objective of economic policy,
there was, *for a very short time,* a notable measure of caution and
moderation among economists regarding the level of employment
which it was sensible, feasible, or desirable to aim at. There

seemed, very briefly, to be some realisation of the danger of
pushing policies directed against the social injustice of unemployment so far as to incur the serious risk of releasing other acute
sources of social injustice, such as inflation or restrictions on
freedom. Pigou, for example, had observed that the result of
maintaining a very high level of employment might be that 'a
spiralling movement of inflation is allowed to develop'.[22]

Keynes in his last fully peacetime pronouncement on policy in
the boom of 1937 had warned against regarding *'even half of the*
unemployed insured persons as available to satisfy home demand:'
and he opposed 'pushing' public expenditure, at that same junc-
ture, *when unemployment was still as high as 11–12%.*[23] In
1944 Keynes considered that Beveridge's target of an average of
3% unemployment might not prove feasible.[24]

Lord Kaldor in 1944 went so far as to assume that the new full
employment objective of 3% would (and should) be combined
with price stability, assuming 'that post-war governments will
pursue a monetary and wage policy which maintains the prices of
final commodities constant . . .' Lord Kaldor then cautiously
added: 'A policy of a rising price level might be incompatible with
the maintenance of stability in the long run'.[25] But the dangers of
the pursuit of the full employment objective creating injustices or
loss of freedom in other directions was, perhaps, most incisively
insisted upon by Lady Robinson. In a paper of 1946 Lady Robinson argued:

> Nor is completely full employment desirable. The attainment of full
> employment, *in this absolute sense* would require strict controls, including
> direction of labour. To raise the average of employment from 86% [the
> average for Great Britain (1921-38)] to, say, 95% would be compatible with
> a greater amount of individual liberty than to raise it from 95% to 98%.
> *To raise it from 95% to 98% (not momentarily — but on the average) would*
> *involve great sacrifices of liberty, and to raise it from 98% to 100% would*
> *involve complete conscription of labour. No one regards 100% employ-*
> *ment as a desirable objective.*[26]

One may not today agree with the precise estimate of the trade-
offs as they were envisaged in the nineteen-forties by Lady Robinson, and it is not clear just whose, or what kinds of, 'freedom' she
held to be threatened by reducing unemployment to 2 or 5%. But
one must certainly admire her cautious and discerning insistence
on the serious costs, or the various forms of injustice, or loss of
freedom, which the pursuit of very high levels of employment
might bring.

However, all this caution and moderation was, among wide sections of opinion, *very* short lived. By the early or middle fifties the trend of public taste for bursts of very high employment, and the politicians' eagerness to meet these tastes (regardless of losses or dangers in other directions) had become clear. 'Growth-manship' also, was beginning to emerge at this stage, and a body of doctrine began to be developed which may be described as 'pseudo-Keynesian'. For, while the Master's magic name was constantly invoked on behalf of the new doctrines, it is impossible to find statements of them in his writings. In fact, it seems fair to regard it as extremely improbable that he would have supported them, in whole or in part, and possibly rather less improbable that he would have applied to them the striking description from his last post-humously published article, when he wrote of 'modernist stuff gone wrong and turned sour and silly'[27] (incidentally, whom *could* Keynes have been referring to?)

A main characteristic of pseudo-Keynesian doctrines was that they followed the tastes of public and politicians in abandoning the former admirable caution and moderation with regard to employment policies and in far-reachingly neglecting the dangers and injustices of inflation and loss of freedom, unlike Keynes who, on the one peace-time occasion when an outburst of inflation threatened the British economy during his life-time, proposed thoroughly drastic measures. There are no grounds for arguing that Keynes would have abandoned his previous caution, or moderate employment targets, because of pressure or unpopularity with politicians and public.

Pseudo-Keynesian policy-doctrines told politicians very much what they had learnt to want to hear. In the twenties and thirties Keynes had repeatedly told politicians and civil servants what they did *not* then want to hear and he had castigated and protested, all in vain, against the policies of Churchill and Baldwin, MacDonald, Snowden and Chamberlain. But in the fifties and sixties the economists who claimed to be 'Keynesian', though sometimes protesting that their policy proposals were not carried to more drastic extremes, were frequently to be found applauding and encouraging governments as they led us on along the road to rampant inflation. What might be called 'life-peerage economics' has seldom criticised inflationary policies on other than party lines, which seems to reduce economic criticism to the level of often irresponsible party-political debate.

Two main pseudo-Keynesian policy-doctrines have emerged and there are no good grounds for supposing that Keynes would have supported either of them.

The first is that unemployment percentages should be pushed down to levels well below what would have been, and were, regarded by Keynes as desirable, e.g. that Beveridge's 3% target was 'obsolete' (Lord Kahn, 1956); or that any target above 2% was 'cold-blooded' and 'out of the question' (Lady Robinson, 1966); or that a target of 0% unemployment should be preferred (Sir Roy Harrod, 1967).

Secondly, on top of the 'full employment' objective, pushed much further than Keynes accepted, the objective of 'full growth', or 'growth in accordance with maximum potential', was to be adopted. It was claimed that this new objective was 'supported by many economists who would claim to have drawn their inspiration from Keynes' (Sir Roy Harrod, 1964). It was also proclaimed that the rate of growth of the British economy could and should be raised by 'comprehensive planning' and 'purposive direction' (Lord Kaldor to the Radcliffe Committee); or that 'we could evidently quickly work up to 6 or 7%', if Britain abandoned her defence effort (Lady Robinson, 1964). Of course, hardly a vestige can be found in the writings of Keynes of the fruitless, pseudo-Keynesian growthmanship which has so seriously aggravated inflation in Britain, especially in 1971-73.

It is clear that views and doctrines which, in fact, Keynes never supported have been described or transmitted as those of Keynes, or as those that Keynes would have held had he lived, or as 'neo-Keynesian', simply in order to make use of the prestige and *réclame* of his name.

Two consequential ideas follow from the two main pseudo-Keynesian policy-doctrines. The first is that price stability must have a minor or very reduced priority as an objective. In fact the 'dangers' were described as those of 'a regime of *stable* prices'; and even advocating the merits of absolute price stability was not only 'dangerous', but 'highly prejudicial to the country's interests' (Lords Kaldor and Kahn to the Radcliffe Committee, 1958, after a decade in which prices had probably already risen faster than in any previous peace-time decade in recorded British history).

Secondly, it was maintained that any tendencies to inflation could and should be countered mainly or entirely by incomes or wages policies. It was a serious 'mistake to suppose that the proper function of monetary and budgetary policy was to secure a tolerable behaviour of prices' (Lord Kahn to the Radcliffe

Committee, 1958). In fact 'incomes policy is the only real remedy' (Lady Robinson, stating 'A Neo-Keynesian View' of inflation, 1974).

The familiar closing words of Keynes's *General Theory* may well exaggerate somewhat the influence of the ideas of economists.[28] But if, in fact, economic doctrines have exercised *any* influence on the course of economic policies in the last 20 years, the doctrines of pseudo-Keynesian economics have, in Britain, been more influential than others, and more responsible than others for the economic position of Britain in 1975. The risk and danger of one kind of injustice — that proceeding from high rates of inflation — has been discounted and disregarded for the sake, allegedly, of reducing, very slightly further, the kind of injustice which reached such appalling dimensions 40 and more years ago. On the other hand, no English economist has written more powerfully of the dangers and injustices of inflation than Keynes, and no one would have more promptly and flexibly switched his attack to the new dangers, or would have been less likely to continue obstinately fighting the last war long after the prime danger had completely changed its nature.[29]

Social justice is essentially multi-dimensional and, outside Utopia, will always be scarce or in short supply. In reasonably free societies and mature democracies, so far as these continue, it will usually, or often, only be possible within fairly narrow limits to reduce some particular form of social injustice for some people, insofar as this is economically determined, by increasing other kinds of social injustice for other people — by diminishing their freedom or by frustrating or disappointing reasonable expectations. At the moment in Britain there seem to be more extreme divergencies of views, a more profound absence of consensus, or, at any rate, more sheer confusion, than at other periods, regarding social justice, both with regard to the distribution of income and wealth, and with regard to 'the right to work' (now increasingly interpreted as the right to hold indefinitely one's present job at whatever rate the power of one's union can achieve, and if this rate results in losses to one's employer the taxpayer must indefinitely meet the deficit).

Social justice is not a subject about which economists as such have any special qualifications for preaching, in terms of trying to lay down which forms of it must have priority over others. On such questions of value economists have no qualifications beyond those they possess as ordinary citizens. Their education, these days, does not usually provide them with any reliable equipment for pronouncing on such issues. Nevertheless, some economists seem to regard political preaching, and the purveying of dogmatic propaganda, sometimes in highly self-righteous terms, as a prime duty.

As it seems to me, however, the tasks to which economists can more suitably direct their energies are massive and difficult enough. First, there is the task of improving factual knowledge, notably about the actual and recent distribution of income and property, which knowledge is now immensely defective. This task requires some minimum of preconceptions and analysis, but *no more than a minimum,* which is *far less* than the speculative abstract 'theories' or 'models' about distribution, to which so much attention has been given since Ricardo.

Secondly, there are the extremely difficult tasks of trying to set out the costs and benefits of attempts to diminish social injustices. Such exercises should not impose particular valuations under the guise of 'measurements', but should rather aim at setting out reasonably, but not, of course, completely fully, the kinds of costs and benefits which may be involved, without seeking to strike some arbitrary balance.

But under these two brief headings, I have simply described just what the papers of Section F, this year, have been seeking so successfully to do.

Notes and references

1 H. Sidgwick, *Principles of Political Economy,* 2nd edn, 1887, p 18.
2 See *Works and Correspondence of D. Ricardo,* P. Sraffa (ed.), Cambridge University Press 1952, vol. VI, pp 210-1, 228, 234.
3 *An Outline of the Science of Political Economy,* 1836, p 2.
4 *Works and Correspondence of D. Ricardo,* vol. V 1952, p 501 (italics added). See also *Markets and the Franchise,* IEA Occasional Paper No. 10, 1966, pp 9-11.
5 *Works and Correspondence of D. Ricardo,* vol. V, p 68.
6 *Principles of Political Economy,* Bk II, Ch 1, Sect. 1.
7 'For Adam Smith, laissez-faire was a programme . . . For the neo-classicals laissez-faire became a dogma' . . . 'Laissez-faire was no longer a programme it became a dogma' . . . 'For fifty years before 1914 the established economists of various schools had *all* been preaching *one doctrine,* with

64   T. W. HUTCHISON

great self-confidence and pomposity — the doctrine of laissez-faire' [v
Joan Robinson and J. Eatwell, *An Introduction to Modern Economics*,
McGraw-Hill 1973; Joan Robinson, *Collected Economic Papers*, vol. IV,
Blackwell 1974, p 61; and *Papers and Proceedings of the AEA*, May 1972,
p 2 (italics added)]. Lady Robinson and Mr Eatwell have been 'preaching
with great self-confidence and pomposity' what is not only an inaccurate
version, but the diametric opposite, of the facts.

8 *Principles of Political Economy*, 1883, p 403.
9 *Official Papers of Alfred Marshall*, Macmillan 1926, p 205 (italics added).
10 *Official Papers of Alfred Marshall*, pp 225-6.
11 *The Times*, 16 November 1909.
12 F. A. Hayek, *The Constitution of Liberty*, Routledge & Kegan Paul 1960,
   p 517.
13 F. Shehab, *Progressive Taxation*, Oxford University Press, 1953, pp 208-9.
   We would remark that Dr Shehab is discussing laissez-faire in distribution,
   and that the 'whole century' of economists' complete 'support' should, on
   the whole, be restricted primarily to the thoroughgoing and very influential support of Ricardo.
14 J. B. Clark, *The Problem of Monopoly*, 1904, pp v and 3 (italics added).
15 Alfred Marshall, *Principles of Economics*, 8th edn, p 518.
16 F. Y. Edgeworth, *Papers Relating to Political Economy*, 1925, vol. 1,
   p 53.
17 Quoted by J. Harris, *Unemployment and Politics, 1886-1914*, Oxford
   University Press, p 119.
18 *Unemployment and Politics, 1886-1914*, p 212.
19 *Unemployment and Politics, 1886-1914*, p 5.
20 *Economic Journal*, June 1975, p 260.
21 *Collected Writings of J. M. Keynes*, D. Moggridge (ed.), Cambridge
   University Press 1973, vol. XIV, p 259 (italics added).
22 A. C. Pigou, *Lapses from Full Employment*, Macmillan 1944, p 72.
   See also for other similar quotations cited below, T. W. Hutchison,
   Economics and Economic Policy in Britain 1946-1966, 1968, pp 28-30.
23 See *The Times*, 11 March and 28 December 1937 (italics added).
24 See Lord Kahn, *Selected Essays on Employment and Growth*, 1972,
   p 103. Incidentally among the assumptions of Beveridge's 3% target was
   that compulsory arbitration would be necessary and that 'in peace in a
   free society, men should not be imprisoned for striking, though they
   may rightly be deprived of all support if the strike is contrary to a
   collective bargain or an agreed arbitration'. (*Full Employment in a Free
   Society*, Allen & Unwin 1944, p 200.) There seems to be no justification
   for Lord Kahn's belief that, had Keynes survived, 'in the light of post war
   experience he would have aimed at an appreciably more ambitious full
   employment target'. Lord Kahn is simply asserting a precise coincidence
   between his own views and what Keynes' would have been had he lived
   longer. There is no valid basis for this assertion. (See 'What Keynes really
   said', *Sunday Telegraph*, 22 September 1974.)
25 See Appendix C to Beveridge, *op. cit.* (note 24) p 398.
26 Joan Robinson, *Collected Economic Papers*, Blackwell 1951, p 106
   (italics added). See also *Essays in the Theory of Employment*, Macmillan
   1947, p 26: 'In general it may be said that *something appreciably short*

of full employment must be regarded as the optimum' (italics added).

27 *Economic Journal*, 1946, p 186. It has been alleged by no less a scholar than Jacob Viner that an attempt was made to suppress the publication of this last article on the ground that it manifested some weakening of Keynes' analytical powers! (See *Keynes' General Theory, Reports of Three Decades*, R. Lekachman (ed.), Macmillan, New York, 1964, p 265.)

28 See *The General Theory of Employment, Interest and Money*, 1936, p 383: 'The ideas of economists and political philosophers, both when they are right and when they are wrong, are more powerful than is commonly understood. Indeed, the world is ruled by little else. Practical men, who believe themselves to be quite exempt from any intellectual influence, are usually the slaves of some defunct economist. Madmen in authority, who hear voices in the air, are distilling their frenzy from some academic scribbler of a few years back.' In recent history surely no more valid (or less invalid) illustration of Keynes' assertions could be found than the dash for growth of 1971-73 'distilled' from the fashionable academic growthmanship of 10-15 years previously.

29 One may not agree with some of Professor Hayek's criticisms of Keynes, but one cannot but concur with his recent conclusion: 'I have good reason to believe that he would have disapproved of what his followers did in the post war period. If he had not died so soon, he would have become one of the leaders in the fight against inflation' (and, it might be added, against pseudo-Keynesian economic policies). See F. A. Hayek, *Full Employment at Any Price?*, IEA, 1975, p 18.

ALAN HARRISON
University of Strathclyde

5 Trends over time in the distribution of wealth*

Introduction

Recent government proposals for an annual tax on wealth have aroused renewed interest in changes in the distribution of personal wealth over time. Indeed, a Royal Commission on the Distribution of Income and Wealth has been established and has recently issued its initial report[2] which concerns itself *inter alia* with just this question. A number of academic writers have expressed the belief that the distribution is moving rapidly in the direction of reduced inequality. Polanyi and Wood, for example, argue that the figures which they present show that 'levelling-up has taken place on a substantial scale' (ref. 3, p 21) and that the process of redistribution is a 'general' one rather than one 'confined to the wealthy' (ref. 3, p 19). Furthermore, they point to evidence which suggests that this redistributive trend has been faster since the 1930s than in the 20 years before and assert that the 'process of change in the shares of personal wealth' since then 'is likely to continue as the incomes of the majority rise further, and as ownership of homes

* This paper is based on work being carried out jointly with Professor A. B. Atkinson (with the support of the Social Science Research Council) which will be reported at greater length in a forthcoming monograph.[1] I would like to thank Professor K. J. W. Alexander, Professor Atkinson and Professor Colin Robinson for their helpful comments on an earlier draft of the paper. Also I am grateful to the Inland Revenue for making available unpublished statistics; they are of course not responsible in any way for the use to which the data have been put.

66

and durable goods, etc., is spread still more widely' (ref. 3, p 20).

Unfortunately, the empirical evidence on which this view is based is inadequate in a number of respects. The official Inland Revenue estimates of the distribution of wealth (ref. 4, table 3) extend only from 1960 to the present so that, in order to make a longer-term analysis of trends over time, use has typically been made of unofficial figures estimated by a number of different authors. While it is unlikely that this will affect the direction of the change it may well affect aspects of the redistribution which are still very important, notably whether the process is actually a general one and also whether, and if so, at what rate, it has increased its pace over time. In addition, without a thorough investigation of the variables which have influenced the distribution of wealth in the past, little can be said about the possibility, let alone the probability, of a continuing redistribution in the future.

This paper therefore addresses itself to these questions. It begins by examining the unofficial estimates made by various authors and assesses the extent to which they were derived using comparable sources and methods. In fact in many respects these estimates differ, which provides a rationale for a later section where an attempt is made to move closer to a consistent series, at least to the extent of making some allowance for the points raised in the next section. This allows us to make a more realistic assessment of the trends over time in the distribution of wealth. Estimates are presented for 29 years between 1923 and 1969 with more preliminary figures for 1970 to 1973, and a brief comparison is made with the series constructed from earlier studies. We then turn our attention to the determinants of changes in the percentage shares of wealth over time, and attempt to identify some of these with the use of regression analysis.

Earlier Studies

This survey is confined to those studies which used the estate method, which multiplies up estate data by the reciprocal of age- and sex-specific mortality rates (the 'mortality multipliers') to arrive at an estimate of the total wealth in the hands of the living population. This method is not without its shortcomings.[5] The choice of multipliers may affect the results; and it may be that the

Table 1   *Main studies using estate method in Great Britain*

Author	Years covered	Area	Population	Type of multipliers
Clay[26]	1911-13	E W	Over 15 and Occupied	GMR for estates under £500; over £500, mortality rates of occupations of a clerical and professional nature.
Daniels & Campion[8]	*1911-3	E W	25 and over	*GMR and SMR based on 1911 D S (intermediate Class I and II as then defined).
	*1924-30			*GMR and SMR based on 1921 D S (intermediate Class I -II (average) and III), unadjusted.
Campion[9]	1911-3 1926-8 1932-4 *1936	E W	25 and over	*As Daniels and Campion.
Langley[14]	1936-8	E W and G B	25 and over	GMR and SMR based on Campion.
Langley[27]	1950-1	G B	25 and over	GMR
Lydall and Tipping[11]	*1951-6	G B and E W	20 and over	*SMR based on 1951 D S for classes I and II (average) adjusted for errors in occupational statements and for unoccupied.

| Revell[28] | 1954 1960 | E W | Over 25 | GMR |
| Inland Revenue (Social Trends)[4] | *1960- present | G B | 15 and over | |

*SMR based on 1951 D S (1960-1963) and 1961 D S for class I-II average above £3,000 (£5,000 after 1969). Adjusted in similar manner to Lydall and Tipping.

Abbreviations: E W England and Wales; G B Great Britain; GMR General mortality rate; SMR Social class mortality rate; D S Decennial supplement.

Table 2 *Distribution of wealth 1911-13 to 1970*

Proportion of adults	England and Wales Adults aged 25 and over:				Great Britain Adults aged 15 and over		
	1911-13	1924-30	1936	1951-6	1960	1965	1970
Top 1%	66	60	56	42	39	34	31
Top 5%	86	83	81	68	64	62	56
Top 10%	90	90	88	79	76	75	70
Top 20%	–	96	94	89	91	89	87
Bottom 80%	–	4	6	11	9	11	13
Original source:	Daniels & Campion		Campion	Lydall & Tipping	Polanyi & Wood		

Source: Polanyi and Wood[3], tables 3 and 4.

Table 3   Percentage shares in total personal wealth 1923-1969

	England & Wales				Great Britain			
	Top 0.1%	Top 1.0%	Top 5%	Top 10%	Top 0.1%	Top 1.0%	Top 5.0%	Top 10%
1923	32.7	61.0	82.2	89.5				
1924	30.7	59.9	81.7	88.6				
1925	32.5	60.2	81.6	88.7				
1926	27.2	56.5	79.5	87.7	not available			
1927	29.6	59.1	80.9	88.6				
1928	26.9	56.0	79.2	87.5				
1929	27.7	54.9	78.6	86.8				
1930	28.7	57.3	79.2	87.2				
1936	22.6	53.0	77.0	86.0				
1938	26.6	54.2	76.8	85.7	26.7	54.4	77.2	86.1
..	..	..	..	..	..	..	..	..
1950	20.5	43.5	68.8	(80.4)	20.2	43.4	68.8	(80.2)
1951	17.1	41.3	68.2	(79.2)	17.0	41.4	68.4	(79.3)
1952	17.4	39.8	65.6	(79.3)	17.4	39.8	65.6	(79.4)
1953	17.1	40.8	66.4	(78.1)	16.8	40.7	66.6	(78.1)
1954	16.4	42.1	67.7	(79.4)	16.3	42.0	67.9	(79.4)
1955	16.7	40.3	65.1	(73.6)	16.2	39.8	64.9	(73.6)
1956	16.9	41.2	67.0	(74.7)	16.4	40.7	66.7	(74.5)
1957	19.8	41.5	65.6	(75.0)	19.3	41.0	65.5	(74.9)
1958	16.1	39.8	65.9	(76.4)	15.8	39.5	65.8	(76.2)
1959	15.6	39.7	65.3	(75.4)	16.1	40.1	65.6	(75.6)
..	..	..	..	..	..	..	..	..
1960	13.7	35.1	60.9	73.4	13.4	35.3	61.4	73.8
1961	15.7	37.7	62.9	74.8	15.3	37.7	63.1	75.0
1962	12.7	33.2	57.9	71.0	12.8	33.8	58.7	71.9
1963	not available				not available			

1964	12.0	33.1	57.8	71.0	12.0	33.5	58.5	71.7
1965	11.8	31.9	56.8	70.3	11.8	32.2	57.5	71.0
1966	11.0	30.3	55.1	69.0	11.0	30.7	55.9	69.8
1967	10.6	30.9	55.1	69.0	10.5	31.0	55.7	69.7
1968	13.5	33.0	57.5	70.8	13.3	33.0	58.0	71.4
1969	10.7	29.7	54.2	65.5	10.6	29.9	54.8	66.4
...	...	...	...	...	...	...	...	...
1970	—	28.2	54.0	65.4	—	28.4	54.6	66.3
1971	—	26.9	52.0	63.3	—	27.1	52.6	64.2
1972	—	29.4	56.3	67.4	—	29.6	56.9	68.3
1973	—	27.3	51.4	63.2	—	27.4	51.9	64.1

Notes: 1. The percentage shares were derived using a log-linear interpolation routine.
2. The figures in brackets are the result of interpolation between very wide bounds and must therefore be treated with considerable caution.

Table 4 *Distribution of wealth 1924 to 1970 (from table 3)*

Proportion of adults	1924-30	1936	1951-6	1960	1965	1970
Top 1%	57.7	53.0	40.9	35.1	31.9	28.2
Top 5%	80.1	77.0	66.7	60.9	56.8	54.0
Top 10%	87.9	86.0	77.4	73.4	70.3	65.4
Top 20%	93.6	92.2	83.6	85.0	85.4	81.5
Bottom 80%	6.4	7.8	16.4	15.0	14.6	18.5

wealth of the dead is not typical of that of the living population of
the same age and sex. In the classification of estates, some of the
'cells' contain very few deaths in any one year, and there may
therefore be substantial sampling error. The estate duty returns
exclude important forms of wealth (for example, assets such as
pensions or annuities which disappear on death, or certain settled
property) and in other cases the method of valuation may be
inappropriate. For these reasons the estate duty estimates have to
be regarded with caution; nonetheless, they provide the best
available source of evidence.

The main features of earlier studies based on estate duty data
are summarised in table 1. From those studies marked with an
asterisk Polanyi and Wood[3] derive a table of trends over time
which is used as support for their claim, already noted, that
wealth has become much more evenly distributed over the last
fifty years; the table is reproduced here as table 2.

There are, however, many aspects of the various studies which
are not comparable, and these may well be sufficiently important
to affect the magnitude, if not the direction, of the observed
changes in the distribution over time. Before considering the
problems of comparability, it is worth noting the effect of the redistribution evident from table 2. While the top 1% has seen a
dramatic fall in its share, the groups below have in fact increased
their share of total personal wealth. Thus, the next 4% below the
top 1% owned, according to these figures, 25% in 1970 compared
with 20% in 1911-13, while the next 5% below them fared even
better, with a share of 14% in 1970 against only 4% in 1911-13.

Turning now to the problems of comparability, the first
concerns the coverage of estate data. Originally these only covered
England and Wales, and all studies prior to that of Langley referred
to this, whereas later estimates referred to Great Britain (for some
intermediate years estimates were given on both bases). This causes
a break in the comparability of the series presented by Polanyi and
Wood as they acknowledge: the estimates up to 1956 relate to
England and Wales, but the later estimates to Great Britain. A
second associated problem of coverage peculiar to 1911-13 is that
the Inland Revenue data did not then distinguish between male
and female descendants and an *ad hoc* procedure was used by
Daniels and Campion to allocate estates by sex. This means that
there is a greater degree of uncertainty surrounding the estimates
for the pre-First World War period. Finally, as can be seen from
table 2, a further break in comparability occurs with the definition

of 'adult' which changes from 25 and over to 15 and over.

The next set of problems concerning the comparability of the studies cited in table 2 relates to the mortality multipliers used. First, the multipliers applied in the year before the Second World War are not fully consistent with those used by Lydall and Tipping in their estimates for 1951-6 or with those used by the Inland Revenue, since the earlier studies used the Registrar General's data on occupational mortality without any adjustment for the un-occupied or for errors in occupational statements. As a result, the social class multipliers were too low in relation to those applied in the 1950's and 1960's. Atkinson and Harrison[6] have shown that this is likely to lead to a lower estimate of the degree of concentration, and hence cause the trend towards equality to be overstated. Secondly, the results quoted by Polanyi and Wood were not in fact those obtained using social class multipliers; they (and Lydall and Tipping) were apparently misled by the presentation of the results in Daniels and Campion, and Campion.[7] The effect of adjusting for this error is to reduce the shares of top wealth groups in 1924-30 and 1936. Again the downward trend is likely to be exaggerated by the figures in table 2.

Another aspect of the studies which has varied over the years has been the proportion of total deaths covered by the estate duty returns and the treatment of the wealth of those excluded. In the period up to the Second World War the estate duty exemption level was £100, and a variety of methods were used to allow for the wealth of those below this level. Daniels and Campion, for example, made an estimate based on the likely value of personal effects and 'working-class savings' for 1911-13 and 1924-30; and Campion did the same for 1936. There are reasons to suspect that these estimates may well be on the low side, and it should be noted in this context that the figures used by Polanyi and Wood were based on the lower end of the range suggested by Daniels and Campion (£28.5 per capita in 1924-30 and £23.30 in 1936). Use of their higher estimates would lead to a fall in the share of the top groups, and a less marked downward trend.[10] On the other hand, the more recent Inland Revenue estimates make no allowance for the wealth of the excluded population, which has the effect of overstating the degree of inequality and understating the trend towards equality.

The above list of problems is by no means exhaustive. For example, I have made no mention of wealth missing from estate duty returns, and in particular the question of whether legal avoidance has increased as rates of estate duty have risen. However, it should be apparent by now that without further research, much care must be exercised in the interpretation of the trends in table 2. In particular, the need for a consistent series of estimates emerges from the catalogue of problems I have discussed and this is attempted in the next section.

Towards a Consistent Series

The series presented here begins in 1923 and extends to 1969, with preliminary estimates for 1970 to 1973. The data for 1911-13 have been ignored because of the special difficulties associated with them noted earlier. On the other hand, the series does include a number of years for which the estate data have not been previously used. Since I have taken great pains to stress the problems of comparability of earlier studies, the main objective here is consistency: a series of estimates based on a uniform method. To this end the approach followed by Lydall and Tipping[11] has been adopted as far as possible. The principal features of the estimates are:

(i) *Coverage*
England and Wales 1923-1973
Great Britain   1938-1973

(ii) *Mortality Multipliers*
Social class mortality multipliers derived from Registrar General's Decennial Supplement, adjusted for errors in occupational statements and for the unoccupied.[12]

(iii) *Wealth of Excluded Population*
Estimates based on balance sheet totals or extrapolation of estate data; estimates for 1923-38 based on Daniels and Campion[8] and Langley.[14] See Atkinson and Harrison[1] for further details.

(iv) *Missing Wealth and Method of Valuation*
The only adjustment made by Lydall and Tipping, (ref. 11, table 3) is that for life assurance. This is not followed here because of the difficulty of obtaining data for earlier years. No allowance is made for pension rights or missing settled property.[15]

The resulting estimates for the overall distribution of wealth

among those aged 25 and over are summarised in table 3 and figure
1. It should be emphasised that, although these are closer to being

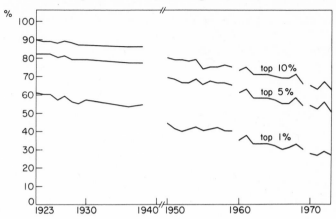

Figure 1

on a consistent basis than the figures quoted earlier, there remain
problems arising from the form in which the estate data are
available. This is particularly important when comparing years
before and after 1960, as from that date the Inland Revenue has
published details of estates below the exemption level which come
to its notice — information that was not previously available. In
the table such breaks in the form of presentation are indicated by
dashed lines, and in the figure they are shown by breaks in the
lines.

The main reaction to the figures in table 3 is to conclude that
there has been a marked fall in the share of the top groups. However, this is not the case when groups below the very top are
considered. For example, although the share of the top 1% has
fallen 31% between 1923 and 1969, the share of the next 4% of
the population below this group has actually risen — from 21% to
24%.[16] Even within the top 1% it is the wealthiest of all, the top
0.1%, which has lost most, since over the same period its share
has fallen by 22% while the next 0.9% has lost only 9% (the
aggregate decline being, of course, the 31% of the top 1% referred
to above).

For years since 1969 I have only preliminary estimates of the
percentage shares of wealth. These were derived by adjusting the
published figures for Great Britain[4] to include the wealth of
those not covered by estate duty statistics and then applying a

correction factor based on the proportionate difference between
these adjusted official estimates for 1969 and those of the consistent series for the same year.[17] The results suggest that my
conclusions, based on the more reliable part of table 3 up to 1969,
hold good for more recent years. Indeed, in 1972 the top 10%
actually held a greater proportion of total wealth than in 1969
although the overall picture is of a slight decline in the share of the
top 1% and relative constancy in the shares of groups below the
top 1%.

I now wish to examine whether conclusions based on table 2 are
still tenable once uniformity has been imposed and a consistent
series estimated. To do this I have constructed table 4 which is
derived from table 3 and additional computations and which,
apart from 1911-13, covers the same years as table 2. It refers to
England and Wales and to adults aged 25 and over throughout but
is otherwise directly comparable with table 2. Where more than
one year is given at the head of a column (e.g. 1924-30) the entry
is the average of the estimates in table 3 for those years.

Looking at table 4 there seems little doubt that the shares of
the top groups have fallen between 1924-30 and 1970. What is
questionable, however, is whether the increasing pace of redistribution implied by table 3 is maintained when a consistent series is
considered. In fact, as far as the top 1% and 5% are concerned it
is not. Dividing the reduction in the share by the number of
years between estimates, table 2 suggests an annual fall in the
share of the top 1% of 0.44% for 1924-30 to 1936, 0.78% for
1936 to 1951-6 and 0.80% for 1960 to 1970.[18] The comparable
figures from table 4 are 0.52%, 0.67% and 0.69% so that the
increase is still apparent but is less significant. If this procedure
is repeated for the share of the top 5% a similar picture emerges.
In this case the annual trend figures are 0.22%, 0.72% and 0.80%
compared with 0.34%, 0.57% and 0.60%. For the share of the top
10%, however, the opposite is true and the average annual reduction is faster in table 4 than in table 2. Thus, in the case of both
the top 1% and 5% the speed of the levelling-up process seems to
be falsely exaggerated by the estimates used to compile table 2.

The next question is whether the redistributive process is a
general one, and to answer this requires examination of the bottom
80%. In table 2 this group increased its share continuously between
1924-30 and 1951-6 and between 1960 and 1970 with the fastest
increase in the most recent time period. When table 4 is considered,
however, the picture is very different. Between 1936 and 1951-6

this group doubled its share of wealth, but subsequently this trend
has noticeably slowed and indeed some regression is apparent
between 1951-6 and 1965. I would therefore argue that the
evidence of a general levelling-up is far less conclusive than has
been claimed.

The summary of the consistent series contained in table 4
indicates that the redistribution of wealth which has taken place
was only in favour of the majority of the population between
1936 and 1951-6. Since 1960 any increase in the share of the
bottom 80% has been attributable at least in part to a restoration
of the position which prevailed in 1951-6. Above this group substantial redistribution appears to have taken place within the top
20% during the same period. If a closer investigation is made,
however, even much of this redistribution is explained purely by a
fall in the share of the top 1%. Each of the groups below the top
1% has maintained or increased its share between 1951-6 and
1970. Furthermore, comparing 1924-30 with 1970 shows that
all of these groups have increased their share, in spite of (among
other things) substantial increases in estate duty.

Is it then the case that estate duty has been the voluntary
tax many have labelled it? Alternatively, have there been forces
working in the opposite direction to prevent a widespread
reduction in inequality? I attempt an answer to these and other
questions in the next section which analyses some of the likely
determinants of trends over time and measures their quantitative
importance.

An Empirical Analysis of the Trends

The estimates presented in table 3 exhibit considerable year-to-
year variation. In part this reflects the sampling error referred to
earlier, and it may therefore be more reasonable to consider
estimates averaged over several years. On the other hand, there
are genuine reasons for year-to-year movements, notably changes
in the prices of assets such as equities and real property, which
are likely to have a significant distributional impact. In this section
I attempt to quantify the effect of these and other factors using
regression analysis. First of all, however, I discuss which variables
I have considered and the ways in which they are likely to
influence the distribution of wealth over time.

The most obvious candidate, of course, is the index of share

prices. In the United States, Smith and Franklin[19] have drawn
attention to the parallel between the changes in the share of the
top 0.5% and the movement in the Standard and Poor's stock
price index, arguing that 'periods when the actual wealth share
was above (below) the trend were generally preceded by periods
of market increases (declines)' (ref. 19 p 164). The importance
of share prices reflects the fact that shares are an asset held disproportionately by the very wealthy. For example, Lydall and
Tipping[11] estimated that in the 1950s 96% of all personally held
shares were owned by the top 5% of wealth-holders. Moving down
the wealth scale, shares are of course held indirectly via insurance
policies and pension funds but it is to be expected that these will
be less sensitive (or at least slower to respond) to movements in
the share price index so that the percentage share of the most
wealthy group and the index is likely to be positively correlated.

A second important influence on the distribution of wealth is
likely to come from the trend towards owner-occupation which is
such a strong feature of the 20th century. Between 1910 and
1970 the proportion of houses which were owner-occupied rose
from 10% to around 50%. In addition, in recent years house prices
have substantially out-paced average earnings with the result that
even if none of the capital on a mortgage has been paid the owner
has still experienced an increase in net worth. Thus the house
price index is a variable whose influence should be tested. Also the
index is, of course, historically important since property was at
one time the preserve of the wealthy, forming a substantial
proportion of their wealth. In consequence, there are likely to be
offsetting forces at work here, with a negative correlation between
percentage shares of the wealthy and the index being the more
likely, the higher is the proportion of owner-occupation.

The next factor which seems at least potentially important is the
level and scope of estate duty, and the extent to which avoidance
took place. As we have already mentioned this was regarded as a
voluntary tax for many years, and it is therefore reasonable to
expect the desire (rather than the ability) to avoid the tax to
increase as rates of duty have increased. On the other hand, some
tightening of the legislation has occurred at the same time and the
net effect is therefore unclear. The position is further complicated
by the nature of the avoidance. Avoidance did not necessarily lead
to property being missed by the estate duty statistics and if this
were the only type of avoidance the estimated distribution of
wealth would remain unequal in spite of estate duty. At the other

extreme if it were all omitted from the statistics, estate duty would have an apparent, but not real, effect.

One important method of avoidance was of course gifts *inter vivos* which were exempt if the donor survived for seven years. Two recent attempts have been made to quantify the effect of this concession, by Whalley[20] and Horsman,[21] and the latter writer suggests that 'the value of gifts made in the late 1960s upon which estate duty was never charged amounted to some £330 million a year; and the duty avoided as a result may have equalled half of that figure or 10% of the net capital value of all estates assessed for duty.' The effect this may have on the distribution of wealth depends of course on the position in the distribution of the recipients after receiving their gifts.[22] Typically these will be just below the donors on the wealth scale (if say a father splits his estate equally between two sons) so that we would expect to observe some limited redistribution within the top groups of wealth-holders. In fact it has been suggested that the increase in the share of the 4% of the population below the top 1% which I noted earlier is the result of just this phenomenon.

The foregoing list is by no means exhaustive but does at least provide measurable variables whose significance can be tested statistically. This suggested a regression equation of the following form (assuming linearity):

$$W_x = a + b_1 S + b_2 H + b_3 Q + b_4 E + \epsilon \qquad (1)$$

where W_x is the share of the top x per cent, S is the share price index, H is the house price index, Q is the proportion of the housing stock which is owner-occupied, and E is some proxy for the level of estate duty. Two additional considerations, however, require the inclusion of four other variables. First, as we noted earlier, breaks in the series in table 3 occur between 1938 and 1950 and between 1959 and 1960. I therefore tested whether these breaks were significant with the use of dummy variables (D_1 and D_2 respectively) which took the value of zero up to the break and unity thereafter. Secondly, it is clear from table 3 and figure 1, and also from the other data series, that there is a strong time trend which would produce spurious results if left undetected. I therefore included time (T) and the square of time as explanatory variables,[23] the coefficient on the latter serving to indicate the rate of change of the time trend. Thus the complete equation was:

$$W_x = a + b_1 S + b_2 H + b_3 Q + b_4 E + b_5 D_1 + b_6 D_2 + b_7 T + b_8 T^2 + \epsilon$$
$$(2)$$

Table 5   *Regression results, England and Wales 1923-1969**

Dependent variable	Constant	Share price index	House price index	Extent of owner occupation	Estate duty	Time	Time²	War dummy	Data change dummy	$\bar{R}^2$	Dw
W_1	73.03 (62.23)	0.07 (2.85)	-0.06 (2.47)			-0.57 (14.33)			-4.07 (3.13)	0.98	2.28
W_{5-1}	3.73 (0.64)	0.03 (1.86)	0.10 (2.04)	0.68 (2.03)	-0.56 (1.71)	0.64 (3.47)	-0.01 (2.97)	3.51 (2.88)	-1.64 (1.59)	0.82	3.08
W_{10-5}	-5.37 (1.16)	-0.05 (2.31)	0.08 (3.25)			0.69 (2.88)	-0.008 (2.53)		4.26 (4.42)	0.82	1.64

( ) : t — statistics

Note: * The estimates for 1970 to 1973 were not used in the regressions because of their preliminary nature.

The data for this regression were for the most part fairly readily available. Given the number of independent variables it seemed sensible to utilise the longest run of years possible for the dependent variable and I therefore used only the series for England and Wales from table 3. Also, to avoid the problems of influences on the share of the top 1% being picked up by a regression which had as its dependent variable the share of the top 5% (which includes the share of the top 1%) I took as dependent variables the shares of the top 1%, the next 4% (5% minus 1%) and the next 5% (10% minus 5%). I ignored the share of the top 0.1% since it is at this level that problems of representativeness in the data become most acute which would, of course, increase the likelihood of spurious results.

Of the independent variables, the share price index and the house price index were straightforward. As a proxy for the effect of estate duty I took the average rate of duty on an estate ten times the level of the average wealth of the population in that particular year. Interestingly, it was necessary to take a multiple of the average wealth figure because in no year was an estate of average wealth liable to duty, although over the period the value of E which I estimated rose from 4% to 18% indicating the considerable rise in the rates of estate duty.

The extent of owner-occupation proved somewhat more problematical. Prior to 1961 tenure type was not a question asked in the census, so that apart from the occasional survey figure information is not available. To overcome this, linear interpolation was used between the 13 observations which were known, yielding a series rising at first slowly from 14.8% in 1923 to 28.6% in 1950, and thereafter rather more quickly, to 49.0% by 1969. It should be added that these figures relate to Great Britain rather than England and Wales, although it is unlikely that this seriously affects the trend in the figures.[24]

Estimating equation (2) using multiple regression analysis produced the results shown in table 5 where the dependent variables are denoted by W_1, W_{5-1} (the share of the next 4% below W_1) and W_{10-5} (the share of the second 5%). In general, a variable which was not significant was dropped from that particular equation, and the regression was re-estimated without it; where this occurred blanks appear in the table. (I was, however, careful to avoid dropping a variable where the insignificance appeared to be a consequence of multi-collinearity.) The estimated coefficients in table 5 provide a number of interesting insights

into the trends over time in the distribution of wealth and in the
remainder of this section I discuss these in detail. Before doing so,
however, I must mention the values of the Durbin-Watson statistic
since these clearly have a bearing on the confidence one can place
in the results. In fact, in the case of the equations with W_1 and
W_{10-5} as dependent variables it is not possible to reject the null
hypothesis that there is zero serial correlation. On the other hand,
the statistic for the equation with W_{5-1} as independent variable
indicates the presence of negative serial correlation so that, for
this reason, the results of fitting this equation must be interpreted
with extreme caution.[25]

The first point to note is that the level of estate duty seems to
have had little effect on the distribution of wealth. The coefficient
on the variable was insignificantly different from zero in all three
equations, although with W_{5-1} as the dependent variable the size
of the t-statistic suggested that it was almost significant and it was
therefore retained. The reason for the poor showing of the estate
duty variable is difficult to establish, given the variety of possible
influences at work. The obvious conclusion — that estate duty has
been of little use as a redistributive agent — is not one I would wish
to draw merely on the basis of this rather crude test. Clearly, a
more sophisticated analysis of the role of estate duty in redistributing wealth is required.

Looking next at the effects of the share price and house price
indices there is an interesting contrast between W_1 and W_{10-5}. An
increase of one point in the share price index is associated with an
increase of 0.07 in W_1 and a reduction of a similar magnitude, 0.05,
in W_{10-5}. Similarly, a one point increase in the house price index
is associated with a fall of 0.06 in W_1 and a rise of 0.08 in W_{10-5}.
In other words, the movements in the percentage share of the top
1% over time caused by changes in these two indices are predominantly offset by movements in the share of the second 5% of the
adult population, with the result that redistribution is again seen
to be rather limited. For W_{5-1}, on the other hand, both indices
have positive coefficients so that the overall effect for the top 10%
is a positive association between the percentage share and both
indices with implied coefficients of 0.05 for shares and 0.12 for
houses. Coupled with a negative coefficient on the house price
index when W_1 is the dependent variable, these results are
broadly in line with what we expect. They do, however, prompt
further thoughts.

First of all, there was much speculation at the time of the

recent stock market fall that this would have a dramatic effect on the distribution of wealth because of the disproportionate holding of shares by the wealthy. The share index was in fact halved in a matter of months which is equivalent to a fall of about 100 points on the share price index I used in the regressions (source: *The British Economy Key Statistics 1900-1970*, page 16). This would lead to a fall in the share of the top 10% of some 5%, given the implied coefficient of 0.05, and leads me to conclude that, at least on this evidence, the impact of share prices on the distribution of wealth is actually far less than is popularly imagined.

A further reflection provoked by the estimated coefficients on the price indices is that the positive relationship between the house price index and the share of the top 10% seems to suggest that owner-occupation is not having a great equalising effect. This was of course tested directly by the inclusion of an owner-occupation variable and the results do seem to indicate the relative lack of importance of this variable. For W_1 and W_{10-5} the variable was not significant while for W_{5-1} there was a positive coefficient of 0.68 implying an increase in the share of this group as owner occupation increases. Superficially, this in turn suggests that the owner-occupiers who are enjoying increases in their net worth as house prices rise are either being lifted into (or are already in) the top 10% of the adult population. Although this does not seem implausible I must add certain reservations about drawing this conclusion purely on the basis of the results in table 5. As I noted earlier, the data series on owner-occupation is rather sketchy and required substantial interpolation especially in earlier years; this may well account for the poor showing of the variable. In addition there is (as I also noted) an offsetting effect between the house price index and the extent of owner occupation and it may well be that once again only a more sophisticated analysis will disentangle the effects.

The final aspect of table 5 which I wish to discuss at length concerns the coefficients on time and the square of time. Looking first at the former, a negative coefficient of 0.57 for W_1 (a downward time trend of a little over ½%) is more than outweighed by positive time trends of 0.64 and 0.69 for the dependent variables W_{5-1} and W_{10-5} respectively, suggesting an upward trend overall. However, the negative coefficients on T^2 indicate that the time trends on both W_{5-1} and W_{10-5} are decelerating. From

$$\frac{\partial W}{\partial T} = b_7 + 2b_8 T \qquad\qquad (3)$$

it is possible to calculate that the trend of W_{5-1} reached a
maximum at $T = 32$ (1932) and the trend of W_{10-5} reached a
maximum at $T = 43$ (1943), thereafter declining until they become
negative at $T = 64$ and 86 (1964 and 1986) respectively. This is of
course a consequence of the negative coefficients on T^2; but the
economic interpretation of the results is more difficult. It is difficult to believe that time itself is the ultimate redistributive weapon
and my belief is that there are other variables whose influence I
have not tested for which time merely acts as a proxy. Once again
then my conclusions are rather tentative.

Conclusion

In this paper I demonstrate that the estimates often used in
discussions of trends in the distribution of wealth are in many ways
not comparable in either source or method. This prompts an
attempt to construct a consistent series which is free of at least
these errors. The series indicates that although the share of the top
1% has fallen quite substantially, groups just below the top 1% have
increased their share of personal wealth so that, at least since 1936,
most of the redistribution which has occurred has been within the
top 20%. The paper then investigates the trends implied by the
consistent series to assess the quantitative importance of a number
of potentially important variables.

The results of this last section, without doubt an analysis fraught
with error, suggest that estate duty has not been a potent redistributive force. Also they demonstrate that falls in the share of the
top 1% are often partially offset by increases in the shares of
groups just below, so that the full effect of the redistribution is
not felt by the rest of the adult population. However, because of
the highly tentative nature of the regression analysis it is as well to
conclude by reiterating how much still needs to be done.

First of all, estate duty affects the estimates of the distribution
of wealth in many different ways and may therefore require a
more sophisticated model to explore fully its influences. Similarly,
the effects of owner-occupation and the house price index, while
being clearly important, need to be identified and measured much
more precisely than I have been able to do. Furthermore, all of
these variables may only work with some lag and this has not been
allowed for in the simple regressions I have estimated.

In conclusion, therefore, it is as well to warn the reader to bear all this in mind when placing his own interpretation on the results of the paper. In spite of all these reservations, however, I still feel that work of this nature is a worthwhile exercise. In the final analysis concern about inequality is a normative affair. A person who does not consider unreasonable a situation where two-thirds of personal wealth is owned by one-tenth of the population, will not feel the need to argue the case for redistributive wealth taxation. But it is better that he has knowledge of the current state of affairs than that there be no information at all, and this paper is, I hope, a small contribution to this knowledge.

Notes and references

1 A. B. Atkinson and A. J. Harrison, *The Distribution of Personal Wealth in Britain*, Cambridge University Press (forthcoming).
2 Royal Commission on the Distribution of Income and Wealth, *Initial Report on the Standing Reference*, Cmnd 6171, HMSO 1975.
3 G. Polanyi and J. B. Wood, *How Much Inequality?* Institute of Economic Affairs 1974.
4 *Estimated Wealth of Individuals in Great Britain 1973*, Inland Revenue 1975.
5 These are dicussed at much greater length in ref. 1, where attempts are made to assess the quantitative importance of many of them.
6 A. B. Atkinson and A. J. Harrison, 'Mortality multipliers and the estate duty method', *Oxford Bulletin of Economics and Statistics*, vol. 37, no. 1, February 1975.
7 In Daniels and Campion (ref. 8, table 23) and Campion (ref. 9, table 13) the social class results are the upper end of the range for the cumulative percentages of persons but the lower end of the range for percentage of capital.
8 G. W. Daniels and H. Campion, *The Distribution of National Capital*, Manchester University Press 1936.
9 H. Campion, *Public and Private Property in Great Britain*, Oxford University Press 1939.
10 Lest it be thought that these are trivial points, it should be noted that this change, together with that relating to the multipliers, could reduce the share of the top 20% from 96% to 92% in 1924-30, thus *doubling* the share of the bottom 80% of the population.
11 H. F. Lydall and D. G. Tipping, 'The distribution of personal wealth in Britain', *Bulletin of the Oxford University Institute of Statistics*, vol. 23, no. 1, February 1961.
12 The multipliers were applied to all estates in excess of the exemption level. In the case of non-dutiable estates which appear in the data from 1960, the multiplier applied was that for the general population, following Revell[13].
13 J. R. S. Revell, *The Wealth of the Nation*, Cambridge University Press 1967.

86   ALAN HARRISON

14 K. M. Langley, 'The distribution of capital in private hands in 1936-38 and 1946-47', *Bulletin of the Oxford University Institute of Statistics*, vol. 12, no. 12, December 1950 and vol. 13, no. 2, February 1951.

15 In the text of their article, Lydall and Tipping[11] make an approximate estimate of the value of these items, but do not allocate them within the top 10%.

16 This is also clear from the relative constancy of the gap between the shares of the top 1% and 5% in figure 1.

17 The share of the top 0.1% was not estimated since the rather crude procedure would probably render it meaningless. Also the official estimates for Great Britain were used to extend the consistent series for both England and Wales and Great Britain, since the figures in table 3 up to 1969 suggest the distinction to be relatively unimportant for the purpose of this analysis.

18 Because of the many differences between the two series in table 2 pre- and post-1960, the trends are considered separately. Hence, I have not estimated a figure for 1951-6 to 1960.

19 J. D. Smith and S. D. Franklin, 'The concentration of personal wealth, 1933-1969', *American Economic Review*, vol. 64, no. 2, May 1974.

20 J. Whalley, 'Estate duty as a voluntary tax', *Economic Journal*, vol. 84, no. 335, September 1974.

21 E. G. Horsman, 'The avoidance of estate duty by gifts *inter-vivos:* some quantitative evidence', *Economic Journal*, vol. 85, no. 339, September 1975.

22 Since some of these people die in any given year it is usually assumed that wealth transmitted as a gift *inter-vivos* is captured in the statistics. However, it is the effect of the gift which is reflected in the estimates in the sense that it is counted as part of the donee's wealth rather than part of the donor's.

23 Alternatively, one can take first differences to overcome this problem and I hope to examine this approach in further work on the subject.

24 On the other hand, the absolute magnitudes of the figures for Britain and England and Wales are likely to differ since Scotland has always had a far lower proportion of owner-occupied housing than the rest of Britain.

25 Use of the Durbin-Watson test suggests that the null hypothesis can be neither accepted nor rejected in the case of both W_{5-1} and W_{10-5}, but by resorting to the Theil-Nagar test it is possible to derive the results given above.

26 H. Clay, 'The distribution of capital in England and Wales', *Transactions of the Manchester Statistical Society* 1925.

27 K. M. Langley, 'The distribution of private capital, 1950-51, *Bulletin of the Oxford University Institute of Statistics*, vol, 16, no. 1, January 1954.

28 J. R. S. Revell, 'Changes in the social distribution of property in Britain during the 20th century', *Acts du Troisième Congres International d'Histoire Economique*, vol. 1, Munich 1965.

C. D. HARBURY
Professor of Economics, The City University, London

5 Equality *versus* mobility in income and wealth distribution

Economic equality with which the Section is concerned this year is one aspect of a wider theme of social justice. The economist's interest in this subject is principally in the allocation of resources among the different members of the community. I do not think that it is possible to consider this narrow aspect of social justice in isolation from the wider so-called non-economic issues, but I shall endeavour to emphasise the more strictly economic ones in this paper.

Distributions of income, or wealth, have two distinct characteristics. The first is essentially a static one and concerns the dispersion of individual incomes about the average. The second characteristic is, in contrast, dynamic and relates to the extent that individuals move up or down the distributions over time. In the argument of this paper I want to draw a sharp contrast between these two characteristics. Indeed my title, 'Equality *versus* mobility in income and wealth distribution', is designed for this purpose. The first of these two objectives, equality, is of course related to the dispersion of individual incomes around the average and is, to an extent, achieved whenever the dispersion is reduced. The second objective, mobility, on the other hand, is not at all concerned with the shape of the distributions but only with the extent to which individuals move up or down it over time.

The question that I wish to raise is whether, at this point of time in Britain, it might be better to move in the direction of greater economic equality or, rather, in that of increasing the

87

mobility of individuals within existing income and wealth distributions. Of course, given complete equality, mobility is pointless.
But if income and wealth are not equally distributed, there is
clearly a case to be argued in favour of policies aimed at increasing
the chances for any individual to earn, for example, an above-
average income, rather than at those which try to make incomes
more equal. Suppose, for example, the same families remain at
the top and bottom of the income and wealth distributions from
generation to generation. Then the pursuit of equality suggests that
the incomes and wealth of the rich should be lowered and those of
the poor raised. But greater mobility would be achieved if rich and
poor individuals changed places from time to time, without
necessarily involving any reduction in inequality of the distribution
itself. I shall examine some of the arguments for increasing mobility rather than attempting to redistribute more equally in the
course of this paper. But it might be said right away that one
reason why such a policy might appear attractive, is that it would
retain some economic incentives, which might assist in increasing
the size of the national cake, not to mention its rate of growth, so
that all the community could potentially benefit in absolute terms.

We cannot reasonably pass judgment on the policy alternatives
of equality *versus* mobility without first examining how far each
of these objectives may already have been achieved in present-day
Britain. I shall shortly refer to some of the evidence on these
matters. Before doing so, however, I should like to ask why
interest in the distribution of income and wealth is currently so
high in this country. My answers to this question provide the first
step in the argument of this paper.

There have, of course, been cycles of interest in this matter.
During the past half-century two periods of interest in reducing
inequalities in the distribution of income have followed each of
the two world wars. A distinguishing feature of each is, I would
suggest, that they have been closely bound up with concern about
the reduction of poverty. Each has also quite quickly given way to
the more traditional concern of economists with the size and
growth rate rather than with the distribution of the national cake.
This is not difficult to appreciate in the light of the experience of
the 1930's and, in the more recent past, with the relatively poor
performance of the United Kingdom in achieving satisfactory rates
of growth of GNP relative to other countries.

The period of the present day is, I suggest, fundamentally
different from those which have preceded it. That is not to say, of

course, that there are no common features. There are two reasons
why I believe this to be the case. One is concerned with a changed
attitude to poverty and the other to the search for an effective
macroeconomic stabilization policy. Let me consider first the
poverty issue. Although poverty, as such, has certainly not dis-
appeared from the British scene, it is perhaps much more closely
contained in identifiable groups, of which that of the old is the
most obvious, than in previous times. Anti-poverty policies are,
therefore, easier to formulate now and they are, to that extent,
more amenable to treatment by other and more direct means than
by attempts at the wholesale redistribution of income and wealth
of the entire population. Moreover, with the long-term trend of
rising living standards, the absolute levels achieved by those below
the poverty line is naturally higher than those of the destitute of,
say, the 1930s, or of earlier times. The proportion of the population
living below the NAB/supplementary benefit line has, for example,
tended to fall during the last 20 years[1] ; and while it is a matter of
judgement as to whether the poverty line itself should rise proportionately with the general standard of living, it is difficult to
avoid the conclusion that society's concern with the elimination of
the deepest destitution is not as strong as it was before.

The decline in interest in the poor *per se* means, I think, that the
current interest in distributional questions is both broader and
deeper than before. To some extent one might even suggest that
the prime concern at the present time is with the shares of the top
percentiles in the income and wealth distribution, but I believe it
goes beyond this and embraces the shares of all income and wealth
groups in the totals. This is, perhaps, no more than a characteristic
of the mass consumption society in which we live, wherein the
majority of the people have come to feel that they have a right to
share to an increasing extent in the good things that life in an
advanced industrial society can offer. As those who identify with
the middle classes rather than with the proletariat seem to have
grown in numbers, have we not entered a kind of emulative society,
in which income groups have increasingly tried to imitate the
consumption habits of those higher up in the scale? Eckhoff[2]
suggested recently that the size of the circle of persons with whom
one compares oneself is important in determining distribution aims.
He, himself, declares that 'if for instance I read in the newspaper
that Onassis had bought a new luxurious yacht, I think no worse
of my little dinghy than I did before. There must be some similarity
and/or proximity before comparisons are made'.[3] Yet it is, I

believe, a characteristic of our society in the 1970s that the range
of persons with whom the average individual compares himself is
an ever widening one. The aspirations of the mass of the people
have become those of what were previously considered the middle
classes. Conspicuous consumption by some of the very rich has
come to generate covetousness and this has extended the area of
interest in income distribution to the entire range.

This leads me to the second important reason for current
interest in distributive questions. We live, unfortunately, in an
inflationary age — one, moreover, in which the old Phillips'
curve, where there is a neat trade-off between growth and
unemployment, no longer applies. This is not the place to discuss
the reasons for the breakdown of the economic relationship
epitomised by the Phillips' curve, but it does appear to be at least
a tenable hypothesis that the militancy, for want of a better word,
of employees and trade unions is partly a function of totally new
aspirations of the majority of working people. Monetarists apart,
this is, of course, why governments of different political colours
and in different countries have attempted to secure acceptance
for prices and incomes policies.

The effectiveness of such policies hangs critically upon securing
their acceptance by trade unions and employers' organisations.
Every formula reflects distributive objectives and until these are
thrashed out in the open and some measure of agreement reached
on them the prospects for long-term success are surely low. I might
add here that conspicuous consumption habits may be more
relevant than high incomes themselves.

The substance of my argument so far, is that the reduced
interest in poverty and attempts to achieve an acceptable prices
and incomes policy has brought into significance, as never before,
the question of the distribution of income and of wealth in its
widest sense. Some would, perhaps, go so far as to suggest that the
very future of a free enterprise capitalist mixed economy may
hang in the balance in the next few years and be dependent on
finding an effective and acceptable package of macroeconomic
and redistributive programmes.

I return to the title of this paper: 'Equality *versus* mobility in
income and wealth distribution'. Starting from the assumption
that we do *not* already have equitable distributions or sufficient
mobility, the issue before us must be to decide the direction in
which the most hopeful movement for success lies. In principle,
there are only four directions: income equality, wealth equality,

income mobility and mobility of wealth. It is time to consider
the extent to which each of these potential objectives has already
been achieved before offering a view on the direction in which
movement should proceed in the immediate future.

In reviewing the evidence on recent major trends, we are
particularly fortunate that the government-appointed Royal
Commission on the Distribution of Income and Wealth, under the
chairmanship of Lord Diamond, published its first two reports in
July 1975.[4] Much debate has taken place over the last few years
on the interpretations which can be placed on the statistical
trends of income and wealth distributions. While the Diamond
Commission has not, of course, managed to extinguish all controversy, its informed opinion is now available on these trends.

What then, we may ask, does the evidence show to have been
the major movements that have occurred? First, let me suggest
that we make a bold assumption and take as read the really
necessary caveats that the Commission and research workers in
this field make before presenting any quantitative results. Most of
the caveats relate to the quality of available data, doubts about
sources and to particular known gaps and omissions. They are, I
believe, adequately set out, both in the report and elsewhere, and
since our only purpose here is to bring out the broadest of trends,
I shall not consider the niceties of the differences in detailed
estimates that follow alternative assumptions to deal with some
of these data deficiencies. I would, incidentally, remark in passing,
however, that I was most impressed with the ingenuity of several
of the alternative calculations of income, and particularly wealth,
distributions that were employed by the Diamond Commission
for their reports. It is of some interest to note that even widely
differing assumptions appear to make remarkably little difference
in the final calculations to most of the distributions.[5]

I am aware that the evidence is still, in spite of Diamond, capable of more than one interpretation. Nevertheless, taking the bull
by the horns I confess to believing that for the period from 1949
to 1972/3 the evidence seems strong that the overall statistical
distributions of both income and wealth have tended to become
more equal.[6] Lorenz curves have moved towards the diagonal and
Gini coefficients have tended to fall. We know, however, that this
does not necessarily imply an increase in the kind of equality that
society particularly wishes to have. As far as income distribution
is concerned, for example, the observed trend towards equality
appears to have been largely the result of transfers of income from

the upper to the middle quantile groups, while the lower half of the distribution has done no more than roughly maintain its share of the total. This statement is, incidentally, unaffected by whether we are talking about the distribution of incomes before or after income tax. Indeed, it is a remarkable and important aspect of redistributionary policy since the Second World War that the effect of direct taxation on the distribution of income appears to have been less important in income levelling than the man in the street might believe. For example, the reduction in the Gini co-efficient between 1949 and 1972/3 for incomes before tax from 41.1 to 37.4 is actually greater than the reduction in the co-efficient for the distribution of post-tax incomes.

Turning next to the distribution of personal wealth, though still notably less equal than that of income, the degree of inequality appears also to have declined substantially over the same, and longer, periods. However, the relevant point here is, perhaps, that the share in the total of the top percentile seems to have fallen proportionately much more than that of the share of the next highest percentiles of the distribution. Moreover, there is evidence to suggest that the percentile groups just below the top 5% have actually increased their share of total personal wealth, mainly at the expense of the topmost percentile. Although there is no firm evidence on the explanation of this kind of transfer, it is at least consistent with the view that is also suggested by other work to which I shall refer shortly, that it reflects a splitting of fortunes more widely *within* the families of top wealth holders, rather than what might be called a 'genuine' redistribution over the whole population.

Let us consider now the implications of these trends in income and wealth distributions, painted with the broadest possible brush, for current policy objectives in the area of social justice. They suggest, I believe, in the first place, that there is not much more mileage for attempting to redistribute personal income through direct taxation. The income tax system of the United Kingdom is, as is well known, not particularly progressive for the great bulk of incomes in the middle ranges. The evidence is also that it has probably become rather less progressive overall, even if only marginally so, since 1949. Such progressiveness as exists in the direct tax system is largely confined to the upper and lower extremes of the income distribution. And it might be added that *effective* progressivity in the top ranges may well have increased without any change in tax rates by such administrative changes as

the filling of tax loopholes and surtax directives. It is at this end
of the distribution, too, that high marginal rates of income tax
are claimed by some to be a major disincentive to effort, though
the evidence supporting this view is by no means definitive. The
machinery of government is involved in extensive and costly
administration of the direct tax system which does not appear in
this country, or in several other countries, to have been a very
effective redistributary instrument. In 1972/73, for example,
direct taxes reduced the share of the top 10% of income groups
from 26.9% before tax to 23.6% after tax. Taxes on expenditure,
moreover, tend to offset such progressiveness as exists in the
direct tax system and, while it is true that the expenditure side of
the government budget is, on balance, redistributive in an egalitarian manner particularly as far as the lowest income groups are
concerned, it is probably true also that the major changes in income
distribution during the period since, say the 1930s, have come in
pre-tax incomes rather than as a result of the government acting as
a direct redistributive agent.[7]

Before drawing further conclusions from trends in income and
wealth distributions, let us turn our attention to such evidence as
there is on changes in the mobility of individuals within each of
these distributions. Here, of course, we are interested not in
changing shares of quantile groups in the distributions, but in the
extent to which individuals move up or down a given distribution
during their lifetime or, at least, comparing their position in the
distribution with that of members of the previous generation of
their own family — for instance, comparing the position of a son
with that of his father. The evidence on this matter, for the United
Kingdom, is notably thinner than that on trends in income and
wealth distributions. As far as income is concerned there is, indeed,
no direct evidence of which I am aware which compares directly
the positions in the income distribution of different birth cohorts
of the same family.[8] If, however, one is prepared to accept that
the categories of the Registrar General's socio-economic classes
are correlated with income, then the work of Professor Glass can
throw some light on the matter. The work that he and J. R. Hall
published 20 years ago provides a bench-mark for more recent
research that he has carried out[9] with data from the General
Household Survey in 1971 and which makes it possible to observe
recent trends between the two dates. Glass's results appear to show
that, broadly speaking and allowing for the fact that there was a
greater increase in non-manual employment opportunities during

the life span of the more recent generation, the pattern of social
mobility has not changed at all dramatically. An apparent
increase in upward mobility is, of course, to be expected with the
expansion in employment in white collar jobs, but the chances
for the sons of those whose fathers were in social classes I or II of
themselves remaining in the same socio-economic group was, in
1971, still very much higher than for those whose fathers were in
lower categories attaining the same status — approximately five
times greater, for example, than the sons of semi-skilled and unskilled manual workers.[10]

In view of the correlation between education and income, an
alternative indirect indicator of income mobility may be provided
by the evidence on the educational achievements of members of
different social classes over time. Work at Nuffield College,
Oxford, also suggests that the social chances of achieving higher
education have become more equal since the Second World War,
though the inequalities of educational chances in the strict sense
have worsened. To take one example, consider the relative chances
of attaining a university education of children from the top and
bottom social groups. In the case of boys born before 1910, about
4½% from social classes I and II entered university compared to
about ½% from social classes IV and V. For the later generation,
born in the 1930's, the percentages had risen to 19 and 1. So,
while higher proportions of children from all social backgrounds
have experienced improved chances of university education, it has
been the middle classes who have taken the greatest advantage of
the expanded opportunities.[11]

Turning next to the question of trends in mobility in the distribution of personal wealth, I can only offer the results of work that
I have been doing, most recently in collaboration with D. W.
Hitchens and P. C. McMahon.[12] The evidence is based on the
proportions of wealthy men in a given generation who were themselves the sons of wealthy fathers. If one accepts an arbitrary
definition of personal wealth as a minimum of £100,000, then one
may take a sample of male top wealth leavers (men dying and
leaving at least this sum) and examine the distribution of fortunes
left by their fathers. This has been done for two samples of men
leaving large estates in the 1950s and 1960s. The results show
there to be no significant differences between the proportions of
wealthy sons who were preceded by wealthy fathers for the two
decades. Over two thirds of both samples of wealthy sons had
been born to fathers who had left at least £25,000 (measured in

constant prices). Most striking of all perhaps is the fact that the
association between the wealth of fathers and sons in both
recent generations did not appear to differ significantly from that
found by Wedgwood for the 1920s.[13] For all three generations of
top wealth leavers, the chances of dying rich were outstandingly
enhanced if one's father had been at least moderately well-off.
Dr. Hitchens and I are currently investigating the pattern of wealth
leaving for a sample of rich sons who died in 1973. Again, one
might expect to observe a decline in the relative advantage of
having a rich father, perhaps indicating only that high rates of
death duty take longer to take effect than might have first been
thought. But many of the fathers of our new 1973 sample died in
the depression of the 1930s when there was, of course, a fall in
the absolute number of people dying rich and this will have to be
allowed for.

This evidence on the continued importance of inheritance in
the creation of personal fortunes in present day Britain may be
seen alongside the previously observed decline in the share of the
top percentile in the distribution of personal wealth and the
increased share of the 6th to 20th percentiles. Together, these
trends really would seem to indicate that mobility in the wealth
distribution has probably lagged behind mobility in income
distribution as suggested by the indirect occupational and educational evidence to which I referred earlier.

This leads me back again to my title, mobility *versus* equality,
and to suggest that it is time to devote more attention to the
former and less to the latter. I shall now assemble my arguments
for so doing, though I readily admit there are probably costs of
one sort or another involved and I shall mention some of them
briefly before I end.

The first reason for being less concerned with making these
distributions more equal is that past policy attempts to do so have
not achieved as much as must have been hoped for. Long-run
changes in income distribution seem to have been caused by what
might be termed exogenous factors, such as rising participation
rates of married women in the labour force, the influence of
inflation and the level of unemployment, at least as much as by
governmental redistributive policies. Also, attempts to redistribute
wealth through, in particular, the imposition of high rates of estate
duty have been to a major extent self-defeating in so far as they led
to the growth of legitimate tax avoidance practices such as gifts
inter-vivos and the use of trusts. Moreover, as I tried to show

earlier, the redistribution of wealth that has occurred has shown up principally in a reduction of the share of the top 1% of wealth holders and has benefitted other wealth groups within the top 10-20%.

I would seriously question too, whether there is much point in effecting merely a shift in the statistical wealth distribution in an egalitarian direction. For example, it would not be too difficult to push the Lorenz curve for wealth a good deal nearer to the diagonal by a policy involving a massive reduction of council house provision on a rental basis. The proportion of owner/occupied housing already rose from 1963 to 1973 from 45% to 52%.[14] And, since dwellings account for a high proportion of total wealth, a major transfer from public sector to private sector ownership of these assets, and to the lower wealth classes who in the main rent council houses, would be highly likely to lead to a more equal statistical distribution of personal wealth. Yet, one is bound to ask whether equality achieved in this way would be really meaningful or desirable. Again, the wealth distribution can change as a result of chance movements, as when the stock market experiences major booms or slumps. It is too early to see what effect the collapse of share prices in 1974 has had on the estimates of wealth distribution that the Inland Revenue calculate using the estate multiplier method. But evidence for the United States showed a decline in the share of the top 1% of wealth holders in National Wealth from 36.3% in 1929 to 28% in 1933,[15] and one might suppose that a similar effect will be observed here. Yet what meaning can be attached to this, particularly if after the recovery, the distribution reverts to its previous shape? What is more important, surely, to know is not whether the share of the top 1% of wealth holders has remained the same but whether it is the *same people,* by and large, who are in the top 1% or whether, perhaps, the crash was an instrument promoting mobility and allowing other groups on a significant scale to replace them.

I do not wish to argue that increases in wealth of the lowest groups is not in itself desirable. Even quite a small reserve can be a great help for someone with virtually no assets — perhaps allowing him to obtain a mortgage for a house or even providing a cushion while he searches for a job. But the fundamental issue about the wealth distribution is surely more than what is reflected in the statistics and is something to do with the distribution of economic power and privilege. I know that concepts like these are difficult to define and, no doubt, even more difficult to quantify, but that does not, I am convinced, mean that they should be ignored.[16] There is little up-to-date statistical information to indicate the broad orders of magnitude in this area. But one might hope that the proposed survey of the Government Statistical Service on the ownership of quoted securities referred to in the Second Report of the Diamond Commission[17] will start to fill this major gap in our knowledge.

Lastly, I must mention one other familiar argument for moving away from a policy of using the tax system to redistribute income towards one for increasing economic mobility. This is the incentive argument. More effective taxation on wealth transfers can allow some reduction in the highest rates of tax, at the margin, on earned income. Moreover, Flemming and Little, in their recent pamphlet on wealth taxation[18] even argue for the replacement of the investment income surcharge by a wealth tax because of the social injustice of taxing what are, in reality, negative investment incomes in an inflationary age. The disincentive effects of high marginal tax rates on effort, risk-taking and saving may never have been definitively established, but I should be prepared to guess that they could be lowered to the benefit of the size of the national cake.

It must now be admitted that a movement in the direction I am suggesting towards less emphasis on equality and more on mobility, might not be wholly advantageous. Here I enter an area where there are few hard facts and where value judgements are, in consequence, paramount. But one imagines that a very mobile society would not be without its own problems. Some of these have been described by Young in *The Rise of the Meritocracy*,[19] but it must not be forgotten that a society in which upward mobility is widespread must inevitably involve the downward mobility of some of the population. The consequent social instability might be very uncomfortable and its costs spill over even to those who are upwardly mobile. I guess that the crucial issue here relates to the speed of the process, though it is easy to over-emphasise this problem if one does not take into account the evidence that the period of time spent in the social class of one's father is, even now, quite low. Using Glass's data for 1949, S. J. Prais has estimated that the average number of generations spent by a family in a particular class was less than two for each of the seven social classes.[20]

A further potentially disturbing consequence of greater mobility that must be faced is that some people may regard the removal of the right of an individual to bequeath or give freely

of money or education to his offspring as tantamount to the loss
of a fundamental freedom. Leaving aside the educational aspects
of this, not because they are unimportant, but because of my
inability to discuss them authoritatively, the major area where
this applies relates to the inheritance of wealth. Spearman has
recently and persuasively pointed to some losses which may
accrue to a society which diminishes inheritance but allows the
concentration of power in government, trade unions and large
corporations to continue.[21] These losses are of independence of
thought and of deed that inherited wealth permits and which can
be, and undoubtedly in the past have been, used at times for
'good'. They may extend, for example, to questions of private
patronage of culture and the arts and the freedom of the press.
There is also a case to be answered of the effect of wealth taxes
on small family businesses and farms, though this one can, I
believe, be answered. It has recently been suggested that there
is a pronounced tendency for family firms to become rigid and
lose vitality when control passes from founding father to subsequent generations.[22] Finally, I should have to admit that the
incentive arguments for switching from income to wealth and
wealth transfer taxation that would favour mobility may be
weaker to the extent that individuals work in order to pass on
benefits to their offspring.[23]

I recognize that these are only some of the potential costs that
may be incurred if one chooses to pursue economic mobility
rather than equality. It must be remembered, however, that the
failure to switch direction also involves costs which many (and I
here include myself) would consider the greater. No one would, of
course, dream of suggesting cost-benefit studies here, so we are
left to rely on personal judgements. I would only remark that,
fortunately, this is not a once and for all 'take it or leave it' situation such as that as to whether or not Britain should or should not
have remained in the Common Market. We can proceed by degrees
and, if at a Fabian rate, perhaps successfully.

Before I conclude, may I just add one further point. It is that I
do not want to give the impression that horizontal equity is no
longer of any importance whatsoever. I only suggest that it is costly,
and probably to a considerable extent self-defeating, to try to
redistribute income much more generally in the direction of
equality. Certain horizontal inequities of a glaring kind do, however, remain and should, I think, be tackled. They include,
outstandingly, the favourable treatment of the self-employed as

against the recipients of wages and salaries,[2][4] the persisting earnings differential in favour of men as against women and the position of owner-occupiers with mortgages compared to those living in non-rent controlled accommodation. These and other cases are still very much in need of action, both through the tax system and by other non-fiscal means.

I conclude by reverting for the last time to my title — mobility *versus* equality. I hope to have produced at least an arguable case for greater emphasis now in Britain on the former. The case rests, first of all, on the basically different reasons why we are currently interested in economic equality in this country compared to those of the past, that is on the relative tractability of the poverty problem today. It rests, secondly, on the need to achieve a set of social distributive objectives acceptable to the majority of the population, if we are to secure a viable macroeconomic policy for price stability, full employment and economic growth. Finally, it is essential to the argument that attention is directed towards mobility as an end in itself and not as a means for achieving more equal distribution.

There are innumerable possible definitions of social justice, so perhaps I should state now, explicitly, my liking for the Rawlsian idea that each individual should assume that he might actually have to change places with other individuals and that those with the same assets of talent and ability should have the same chances of success, regardless of their initial place in the social system.[25] Both ideas tend to move me to favour more mobility, at least after the achievement of a degree of equality. I have tried to argue that we are now approaching the area of diminishing returns to equality policies, particularly in so far as income is concerned and that, although there are certainly costs and risks involved in changing direction, the greater need at the present time is for more economic mobility.

Notes and references

1 A. B. Atkinson, *The Economics of Inequality*, Oxford University Press 1975, p 194.
2 T. Eckhoff, *Justice: Its Determinants in Social Interaction*, Rotterdam University Press 1974.
3 *Justice: Its Determinants in Social Interaction*, p 285.
4 Royal Commission on the Distribution of Income and Wealth, Report No. 1: *Initial Report on the Standing Reference*, Cmnd 6171 and Report No. 2: *Income from Companies and its Distribution*, Cmnd

6172, HMSO 1975.

5 An outstanding exception to this is perhaps the effect of inclusion or exclusion of occupational and state pension rights to the shares of quantile groups in the distribution of personal wealth.

6 Though unquantified at present there is some reason to believe that allowance for non-pecuniary advantages of different occupations would show greater equality of income distribution than the published statistics. Allowance for fringe benefits, however, might work in the opposite direction.

7 There are, however, shorter periods within which it may have become marginally more progressive.

8 There is evidence to suggest that income distributions which allow for year-to-year fluctuations in individual incomes tend to be more equal than distributions based on a single year.

9 D. V. Glass (ed.), *Social Mobility in Britain*, Routledge & Kegan Paul, 1954, ch. 8.

10 I am grateful to Professor D. V. Glass for providing me with this information in advance of publication.

11 A. H. Halsey (ed.), *Trends in British Society since 1900*, Macmillan 1972, ch. 6.

12 C. D. Harbury, 'Inheritance and the distribution of personal wealth in Britain', *Economic Journal*, vol. LXXII, 1962; and C. D. Harbury and P. C. McMahon, 'Inheritance and the characteristics of top wealth leavers in Britain', *Economic Journal*, vol. 83, no. 331, 1973.

13 J. Wedgwood, *The Economics of Inheritance*, Routledge 1929, ch. 6.

14 See first report of the Diamond Commission, para 100.

15 J. D. Smith and S. D. Franklin, 'The concentration of personal wealth, 1922-1969', *American Economic Review*, vol. LXIV, no 2, 1974.

16 For similar reasons I find it difficult to accept that the inclusion of state and occupational pension rights as part of personal wealth (which, of course, lead to significantly lower coefficients of inequality) show a more relevant picture of wealth distribution for the purposes of policy formulation to achieve 'social justice'.

17 Second report of the Diamond Commission, para 300.

18 J. S. Flemming and I. M. D. Little, *Why We Need a Wealth Tax*, Methuen 1974.

19 M. Young, *The Rise of the Meritocracy*, Thames & Hudson 1958.

20 S. J. Prais, 'Measuring social mobility', *Journal of the Royal Statistical Society*, series A, vol. 118, P & I, 1955. Mobility tends, of course, to be greatest into neighbouring social classes and a broader grouping to fewer classes would tend to raise the average time spent in the class, but the figures are still surprisingly low.

21 D. Spearman, *New Society*, 20 February 1975.

22 J. Boswell, *The Rise and Decline of Small Firms*, Allen & Unwin 1972.

23 I also fear that the closing of many loopholes that the Capital Transfer Tax has brought about may induce some people to switch from avoidance to evasion.

24 The share of income from self-employment in total personal income rose by about 15% in the ten years ending 1973 (first report of the Diamond Commission, para 99). It remains to be shown that recent changes in their

tax and national insurance treatment offsets their notably more favourable treatment *under income tax* than wage and salary earners.

25 J. Rawls, *A Theory of Justice*, Oxford University Press 1971. In the context of increasing mobility the concept would need to be reformulated so as to refer to the position of one's heirs relative to oneself. (For reasons which are partly obvious and partly because I am not at all sure about the ease of identifying the least advantaged groups, I have yet to be persuaded by his maximin criterion for the achievement of distributive equity.) See the papers on 'Concepts of distributional equity' by Rawls, Mueller and Buchanan and Bush, *American Economic Review*, vol. LXIV, no. 2, 1974.

CEDRIC SANDFORD
Professor of Economics, University of Bath

7 The taxation of personal wealth

Introduction

In a previous paper Mr Harrison examined the distribution of personal wealth in Britain. Despite the imperfections of the statistics and the difficulty of interpreting them, many people would argue that the overall message is clear — the distribution of wealth in Britain is unacceptably uneven. For those who make that value judgement it is a short step to the proposition that we should tax wealth as one means of reducing that inequality.

To say that we should tax wealth in order to reduce the inequality in its distribution is a deceptively simple statement. If policy is to be rational we need to look at different forms of taxes on wealth and at their different costs and consequences.

Forms of Wealth Tax

We can distinguish two categories of tax on personal wealth — wealth transfer taxes and taxes on the stock of wealth. Wealth transfer taxes are levied when wealth passes from one person to another, as by gift or legacy. A capital gains tax, levied on the realisation of an asset, might also be included in this category. Wealth transfer taxes are necessarily levied at irregular intervals; and the tax liability is related to the nature of the transfer and hence to the source of the wealth — gift, inheritance, capital gain.

The other category of wealth tax — taxation of the stock of

wealth — consists primarily, if not exclusively, of the tax which, in current usage, has attracted to itself the label 'wealth tax'. Although wealth taxes are sometimes (as in Germany) levied on companies as well as persons, or (as in Spain) on companies only, they are usually confined to persons. Unlike wealth transfer taxes, they are levied regularly, usually annually. Just as a tax on realised capital gains might properly be regarded as a wealth transfer tax, so a tax on accrued capital gains, levied regularly, might be regarded as a form of wealth tax on the stock of wealth. But to the best of my knowledge, an accrued capital gains tax nowhere exists in practice and we shall say no more about this theoretical possibility. In this paper we shall follow current UK practice and use the term wealth tax to mean an annual personal net wealth tax.

Unlike a wealth transfer tax, an annual wealth tax takes no account of the source of the wealth. Whether the wealth was acquired by inheritance, by gift, by capital gain, by a win on the pools, or by hard work, enterprise and saving, a wealth tax treats all forms of wealth identically.

There are two other important differences between wealth transfer taxes and an annual wealth tax. The transfer of an asset, often, though not invariably, generates a valuation for purposes other than taxation but which can then be used as the tax valuation (e.g. a valuation of the deceased's property is often required at death to implement a will). Further, a wealth transfer is often associated with a flow of funds, which may facilitate tax payment. A wealth tax is never associated with a valuation required for other purposes; nor is there any flow of funds. Consequently, a wealth tax is more likely to give rise to administrative problems causing additional costs to the Revenue and the taxpayer, and a heavy wealth tax may generate liquidity problems for the payer. At this point a word of warning is appropriate, however. We must beware of assuming that a wealth tax is necessarily paid out of wealth, i.e. by a disposal of assets. The adjective 'wealth' refers to the tax base. It tells us nothing of the source of payment.

Wealth Transfer Taxes

The key wealth transfer tax is a death duty; a gift tax can be regarded as a necessary support to a death duty to prevent avoidance. Death duties themselves can take various forms and the fundamental distinction is between the estate duty and inheritance tax forms. With an estate duty, tax is levied on the total estate left by the deceased irrespective of its distribution, so that the same tax is paid if a millionaire leaves all his property to one son or divides it amongst one hundred persons. The inheritance tax, on the other hand, taxes what is received irrespective of the size of estate from which it comes. Tax is related to benefit received.

As Winston Churchill once put it, an estate duty is an attempt 'to tax the dead instead of the living.' Taxing the dead would be a good idea if you could do it – but you cannot. A death duty deprives heirs of property they would otherwise have had. In the absence of good reasons to the contrary it seems logical to align the liability with the incidence of the tax. The point has been put succinctly by Professor Lord Kaldor:[1]

> Death duty is a periodic levy on property falling on the person or persons who inherit a man's estate. The legal notion that the estate duty is a tax on the deceased is really nonsensical – though it may have had rather more justification in the old days when people saved specially during their lifetime to cover death duty liabilities on their decease. If the incidence of estate duty is really on the legatee and not the testator, the sensible thing is to recognise this and to impose a tax on the recipient.

The Capital Transfer Tax (CTT), as introduced in the United Kingdom 1974-5, is an extension of the estate duty principle so as to include gifts and to tax on a cumulative basis. A donor is allowed certain tax-free gifts each year. These apart, the gifts he makes are clocked up and recorded against him. Tax starts to be paid at progressive rates when the cumulative total (using current UK figures) exceeds £15,000, the life-time exemption. To determine the rate of tax appropriate to any gift, all gifts are cumulated; and to determine the appropriate tax at death the cumulative total of gifts is added to the estate left at death. The correspondingly sophisticated version of the inheritance tax is an Accessions Tax (AT): a tax levied on the beneficiary of a legacy or gift, the tax on any one receipt being determined by the total amount received by way of legacies and gifts. It is thus similar to a CTT with a vital difference that it is levied on the transferee instead of the transferor.

Before comparing the effects of CTT and AT, particularly on the distribution of wealth, let us briefly glance at some of the features of the CTT in the UK – features relevant to the comparison with an AT, but not all *necessary* features of a CTT.

First, let us look at the method of taxing gifts. In determining the appropriate rate of tax gifts are 'grossed up' so that the tax as well as the gift determines the tax rate. Let us take an example. Suppose the effective (or average, as distinct from marginal) rate of tax on a transfer of £100,000 is 25% and on a transfer of £200,000 is 50%. If I want to make a gift of £100,000 to my son I have not, as might be thought, met my tax liabilities if I pass over £25,000 to the Revenue at the same time as I hand over £100,000 to my son. To determine the tax due the gift has to be grossed up to that figure which, after deduction of tax will leave £100,000. In this example the grossed up total would be £200,000 which, at a 50% rate, leaves £100,000 as the net gift and provides the Revenue with £100,000.

The logic of this procedure is that it accords the same treatment to transfers *inter-vivos* as to transfers at death. If I died leaving £200,000, tax would be levied on that sum, and, if the effective rate was 50%, then the heirs would get £100,000 and the Inland Revenue would get £100,000. 'Grossing up' gifts is necessary to put the taxation of gifts and estates on a par.

Now, however, comes a peculiarity. As originally proposed in the White Paper and the Finance Bill, the tax rates for life-time transfers and for transfers at death were the same. Then, at the end of the Committee Stage, the Government introduced an amendment to the Finance Bill which provided for lower effective rates for life-time transfers. Thus, having taken on board all the complications of grossing up in order to establish the principle of equal taxation of gifts and estates, the Government then went back on the principle; the reason given was the need to aid small businesses and farms — although the lower rate schedule applied to all gifts.

We shall say something on the validity of this argument later when we examine the economic consequences of heavy death duties. For the moment let us note another unfortunate consequence of it. One of the least satisfactory features of the former estate duty was the gifts-*inter-vivos* provision. In the absence of a general gift tax, the estate duty was supported by a provision which laid down that gifts made within the seven years before death should be aggregated with the deceased's estate for estate duty purposes. This provision generated serious inequities. Tax could be avoided by the relatively simple process of giving property away and living for seven years. But not everyone was equally well placed to make gifts. Moreover, the responsibility

for taking avoiding action rested on one person, the penalties
for inaction were incurred by another. Thus, if a wealthy parent
was mean, lethargic, procrastinating, patriotic, took a sanguine
view of his life expectation or held property in a form which did
not readily lend itself to giving, the heirs suffered.

The tax treatment associated with premature death was
particularly harsh. Suppose two men of the same age and
circumstances make gifts to their children at the same time: one
survives seven years and thus no tax is payable on the gifts, the
other falls under a bus on his way from the solicitor's office;
estate duty is immediately liable on the gifts, which are aggregated
with the estate. This difference in treatment of gifts is inequitable;
indeed, it could be argued that if there was to be any distinction
it would be more justifiable the other way round, for the heirs of
a person who dies prematurely are more likely to need favourable
tax treatment than the heirs of the longer-lived. In short, the gifts-
inter-vivos provision represented a state-created incentive for the
wealthy to engage in a gamble of a peculiarly sordid kind — a
lottery with length of life, a dice with death, the state standing
ready to step in and tax, not the gamble as such, nor the winners
of the gamble, but the losers — or, more accurately, the unfortunate heirs of the unfortunate losers.

Moreover, under the estate duty regime it was probably the
richest who were best able to take advantage of such avoidance
opportunities: they could afford the best advice; could give
without impairing their living standards; and, in so far as their
wealth was inherited, they would often be better placed to give
early, thus increasing the chance of successful avoidance.

One of the attractions of extending the base of estate duty to
include all gifts was to get rid of these inequities. But the introduction of a lower rate of duty on gifts has meant that measures
had to be taken against gifts made 'in contemplation of death'. So
an *inter-vivos* provision had to be introduced into CTT. This time
the period is three years. The inequities thus still continue,
though in a less acute form.

The second feature in the CTT we should note is that it provides
for all transfers between spouses, whether during life or at the
death of one of them, to be tax free.

Let us now return to our main theme — the comparison of
different forms of wealth transfer tax, especially from the viewpoint of reducing inequality in the distribution of wealth.

An AT can be expected to be more effective than an equivalent

CTT in reducing inequalities in the distribution of wealth for two main reasons. First, it is large receipts that perpetuate inequality and an AT therefore strikes at the heart of the matter. Second, an AT provides an incentive for wealth holders to disperse their property and to give or leave it to those who have received little by way of gifts or legacies; by so doing wealth holders reduce the total tax paid and thus themselves determine the disposal of a larger part of their wealth. Both of these points require elaboration.

Large estates left at death, or a large aggregate of life-time gifts, only perpetuate inequality in so far as they involve large receipts by heirs or donees (especially those who have already received substantial legacies and/or gifts). The CTT therefore puts the emphasis entirely the wrong way round. Ignoring for the moment the effects of earlier accessions received by the beneficiary, an AT which was *equivalent* to CTT would tax estates left to one or a small number of people more heavily than CTT, and estates which were widely and evenly dispersed less heavily. We can define equivalence between CTT and AT as a situation which, *for any given disposition of property by gift and at death,* would bring in the same total revenue by either tax. This means, for example, that if one were devising an AT scale equivalent to any particular CTT, the rates (but not the overall tax burden) would be higher; the rate structure would be devised such that, if the distribution of property by gift and legacy remained unchanged, the same total revenue would accrue; however, its incidence would have changed — sole inheritors would pay more whilst the aggregate tax paid by inheritors of a widely and evenly dispersed estate would be less.

In fact we should not expect the disposition of property by gift and death to remain the same if an equivalent AT replaced CTT because of the second way an AT promotes equality — through its incentive to disperse. It is, of course, true that that incentive is likely to operate most strongly within family groups and thus it may be queried whether a reduction in inequality brought about in this way will be very meaningful. But given the rate structure of an AT, wealth holders can only keep the tax bill down by dividing their wealth within a large rather than a nuclear family. This is particularly so with wealth holders with one child, especially if without grandchildren. Moreover, there are many holders of substantial wealth who have no children. In so far as an AT leads to a diffusion of wealth within families, but outside the nuclear family, this is surely a meaningful redistribution.

When account is taken of multiple gifts and legacies the

superiority of an AT over CTT as a means of reducing inequality
of wealth is still more pronounced. Suppose, for example, that
(father) A and (uncle) B, neither of whom had made previous
taxable gifts, each left £200,000 to C. Then under CTT the combined duty paid would be double the amount due on £200,000, a
total, at present UK scales, of £169,500. Under an AT, C would
pay at the rate appropriate to £400,000. Even with the same rate
structure as CTT (and an equivalent AT would have a higher rate
structure) the tax paid would be £204,750. If C had received
previous gifts and legacies the tax would he higher still.

To sum up: an AT equivalent to CTT is bound to be more
effective in reducing inequality of wealth than CTT. In so far as
people do not alter the disposition of their property, the same
revenue is received by the state but more of it comes from the
wealthy and less from the less wealthy; in so far as wealth holders
do change the disposition of property under the influence of the
tax, this will act directly to reduce inequality by favouring those
who have received little by gift and legacy at the expense of the
big recipients.

Whilst the effect on inequality of wealth is the principal point
at issue, other considerations might be briefly indicated. An AT
has advantages of equity over CTT. CTT provides for the exemption of transfers between husband and wife irrespective of their
circumstances. An AT can contain the same provision if desired,
but offers scope for much more flexible adjustments to the
circumstances of the beneficiary. Thus an AT can readily provide
for special exemptions for legacies received by a minor child from
a deceased parent (e.g. as in the Swedish inheritance tax, an
exemption can be given for each year by which the child's age
falls short of majority).

Further, an AT avoids the misunderstanding and the mathematical complications associated with the 'grossing up' of gifts.
Under AT, gifts and legacies in the hands of the recipients are
taxed on precisely the same basis. On the other side, an AT would
be more expensive to administer than CTT because there would be
more beneficiaries than donors (during life and at death) so that
more records would need to be kept. But the effect of this additional administration can easily be overstated. Experience with
estate duty demonstrated that the heaviest costs of administration
related to claims to duty in complex situations and where there were
difficult valuation problems associated with particular categories
of property — land, private companies, valuable personal chattels.

Administration of an AT should involve little or no increase in this
kind of work for we are only dealing with the same amount of this
kind of property. The vast bulk of the extra work which an AT
would impose relatively to CTT would be of a routine nature. By
appropriate administrative methods, including computerisation
and the use of national insurance numbers to aid identification in
retrieving records, there is no reason to believe that costs could not
be kept within the customary limits of the Inland Revenue.[2]

There is one other important difference between CTT and AT;
the two forms of duty imply a different political and social philosophy. CTT reduces inequality by appropriating private assets to
the state. An AT works partly in this way but also it works by
encouraging property owners to make gifts or bequests to those
who have received little or nothing by way of previous accessions.
Thus the philosophy of CTT is more akin to ideas of state socialism;
the AT has more in common with a private enterprise or mixed
economy and leaves more choice to the individual.

What of the economic effects of heavy death duties? Is there an
economic cost of using death duties to reduce inequality of wealth?
In making our assessment we must acknowledge a degree of
ignorance. Much research needs to be done in this field. But we can
say something. There are two aspects which require particular
consideration: the effects on saving and hence, given investment
opportunities, on the rate of investment; and the effect on the
private business including agriculture.

In considering the effects on saving we must distinguish between
the incentive and the capacity to save, and between the effects on
the property accumulator and on heirs. The desire to bequeath is
only one of many motives for saving and much saving is under-
taken with no thought of bequests in mind, e.g. saving for future
security and enjoyment, for the power and status that wealth
confers, for the posthumous glory of dying rich, for the desire to
manage a large business, and saving from the sheer inability to
spend one's wealth, and many others.

Empirical data about the motives for saving are lacking in this
country, but some American studies suggest that whilst the desire
to make bequests is an unimportant motive for the population as a
whole, it is more significant the higher the income group.[3] Further,
it is a motive which may grow in importance with the age of the
property accumulator, when some of the other motives for saving
have been fulfilled or have become impossible of fulfilment.

However, even if the desire to bequeath has become the

dominant motive for saving for such older wealth holders, it does not follow that they will react to heavy death duties by saving less. They might even be induced by the tax to save more: if they want to pass on to their heirs a given capital sum to provide them with a given future income, they must save more to achieve this objective. In any case, as Professors Rolph and Break have pointed out: 'By the time people have reached the age when estate considerations weigh heavily they have also reached the age when radical departures from previous modes of living are generally unwelcome.'[4]

If theory is inconclusive, it is particularly difficult to try to establish the outcome by reference to empirical data relating to the past effects of estate duty, for those with the strongest desire to bequeath were able to go a long way to attain their objectives by means of avoidance.

If the effect on the saving of property accumulators is unclear, the effects on the saving of the heirs, potential and actual, are clearer as to direction (although not extent). Both by reducing their expectations and their actual inheritance, a death duty is likely to stimulate saving by heirs.

The effects of estate duty on the *capacity* of an accumulator of wealth and of an inheritor to save are more straightforward than the incentive effects. The capacity of an accumulator for work, saving or enterprise is unaffected; death duty does not *require* him to alter his work effort or savings pattern. The death duty does, however, reduce the capital of the inheritor below what it otherwise would have been, restricting his capacity for future saving. A heavy death duty particularly reduces private saving in the sense that the deceased need have made no provision for meeting the tax and the inheritor will probably regard only the post-tax inheritance as his capital and will also make no attempt to meet the tax, wholly or partly, by reducing his consumption. A heavy death duty is thus a tax assessed on capital or wealth and almost entirely paid out of wealth. The payment of death duty involves the transfer to the government of assets which can suitably be applied to debt redemption or other capital account purposes. Provided the government uses them in this way (and government accounts currently recognise the distinction) the effect is to reduce the total of accumulated private saving but correspondingly to increase public saving.

Let us turn to the second relevant feature — the effect of death duties on the private business, including its effect on agriculture; this is the aspect of capital transfer tax which has attracted much attention and led to the introduction of the lower schedule of rates for lifetime transfers.

Space precludes any full treatment of this subject, but the general argument is that on the death of a sole proprietor of a business or an owner-occupier in agriculture, or of a major shareholder in a private company, payment of duty endangers the efficient running of the concern, e.g. the duty may result in a burden of debt which restricts the firm's growth; farms may be fragmented when parts are sold off to pay duty; a business may have to be sold in whole or in part.

Undoubtedly, these kinds of difficulties do occur for private firms and owner-occupied farms, but it is less clear that the economy as a whole suffers. There is nothing in the process of inheritance that ensures that the son of a businessman or farmer is necessarily the best person to carry on his father's enterprise. There is something to be said for property coming onto the market fairly frequently, for there must be a *prima facie* assumption that the person or organisation prepared to pay the best price for it is able to put it to the most efficient use. If private firms provide a source of vital innovation in the community, it is equally true that they also include in their number some of the least efficient business organisations; and sales of such firms, forced by death duty considerations, may increase, rather than reduce, the efficiency of the economy. Further, some recent research by Jonathan Boswell[5] has suggested that the importance of the dynastic motive for building up new enterprises may have been much exaggerated.

For a variety of reasons — the ownership structure, the enormous inflation of land prices in recent years and the lack of special financial facilities (such as the Estate Duties Investment Trust) — the position of the owner-occupier in agriculture faced by heavy death duties is probably more difficult than that of a firm in industry or commerce. But in assessing these difficulties, we should bear in mind the concession which 'full-time working farmers' enjoy under CTT by which their land is not valued at its open market capital value, but as a multiple of an assessed rental; and the provision by which duty on industrial or agricultural assets can be paid in instalments over eight years.

Whilst we lack evidence, it cannot be taken as axiomatic that a heavy death duty must have a detrimental effect on an economy. This is particularly true when the death duty takes the form of an AT rather than a CTT.

With an AT there is one method of reducing the effect of death
duty on a business not open to wealthy businessmen under CTT —
the owner can transfer shares in the business to people who have
received little by way of previous gifts and legacies. Of course,
there will be many occasions where this procedure will be inappropriate, but in other cases, for example when there are senior
employees of established ability and interest in the firm, it may be
so. At least an AT offers an option for reducing tax by this means
not available under CTT.

Further, the diffusion of property in the private sector, which
characterises the operation of AT as against CTT, may widen
business opportunities. The Bolton Committee recognised that
the inheritance form of death duty might have this effect: 'It is
possible that the adoption of a system of legacy duties would
benefit the small-firm sector by causing capital to be more widely
dispersed in small units and thus giving more people the means
of starting their own businesses.'[6]

Annual Wealth Tax

In considering the annual wealth tax the vital distinction concerns
not its form but its rates. We can distinguish on the one hand a
wealth tax which, together with income tax, can be met out of
income. This, in a convenient shorthand, we can call a 'substitutive'
wealth tax. On the other hand, there is the tax set at such a level
that it is impossible for the wealthy to pay income tax and wealth
tax combined except by disposing of some of their assets. This we
can call an 'additive' wealth tax. Any particular wealth tax may be
partly substitutive or partly additive; although the distinction lacks
precision it is useful.

Wealth taxes on the European Continent (which exist in about
ten countries) are all of the substitutive variety. They are supplementary income taxes akin to our investment income surcharge.
That they are capable of being paid from income and intended to
be so paid is clear from the prevalence of special 'ceiling'
provisions which exist in those countries where income tax and
wealth tax are heaviest (e.g. Sweden, Norway, Denmark and the
Netherlands). Although the provisions differ in their detail and
complexity, the general intention is to provide that combined
income tax (including local income tax where applicable) and
wealth tax should not exceed a prescribed percentage of a taxpayer's income. In the Netherlands the percentage is 80, in Sweden

it is 80 up to a certain income band and 85 above that level, and
in Norway the figure is 90.

The Green Paper proposals of the Labour Government are
compatible with a wealth tax that lies anywhere between the
wholly substitutive and the wholly additive. The only firm commitment of the Government is to the principle of a wealth tax.
Two schedules of rates are given in the Green Paper but we are
specifically warned that both are 'merely for illustrative purposes'.
Investment income surcharge may (or may not) be allowed as an
offset to wealth tax; as the Green Paper puts it: 'The Government
. . . will consider limiting . . . liability to whichever of them is the
higher'; and there is a hint in the Chancellor's Foreword of a
possible reduction in income tax when wealth tax is introduced.
The 'possibility' of a ceiling provision along Continental, or on
somewhat different, lines is envisaged. The way the decisions go on
these issues will determine the weight of tax imposed. Our only
guide is the stated objectives of the tax set out by the Chancellor
in his Foreword — to supplement income tax by taking account of
the additional taxable capacity conferred by wealth over and
above any income derived from it, and to reduce inequalities in
the distribution of wealth.

The most obvious way of using a wealth tax to reduce inequality
of wealth is to impose it at rates such that, taken in conjunction
with income tax, the wealthy can only pay it by disposing of their
assets i.e. an additive wealth tax. Inequality is then continuously
reduced; each year there is a reduction in the proportion of wealth
held by the biggest wealth holders.

However, this reduction in inequality may be gained at a heavy
economic cost. There are good reasons for considering that
combined income tax and wealth tax at this level would have
seriously harmful economic consequences. These can be briefly
outlined as follows.

1. *Damage to incentives to enterprise and saving and, indeed, a
stimulus to consumption spending by the rich.* At marginal tax
rates[7] over 100% (as they would have to be if the wealth tax was
to operate directly to reduce inequality), attempts to save at best
simply reduce the rate at which personal wealth declines. Let us
illustrate this by a very simple if slightly naive example using
figures related to the Green Paper proposals. Suppose a person
with £1 million wealth receives a £2,000 legacy from Aunt Jemima.
If he invests it at 5% the income would be £100. Income tax

would take £83; investment income surcharge, if still applied, would take £15; wealth tax at 3% would take £60, totalling £158. The combined marginal rate of income tax and wealth tax would be 158%, or 143% without investment income surcharge. If the legacy had been invested at 10% the combined marginal rate of income tax and wealth tax would be 128%, or 113% without investment income surcharge.

Each year the wealth holder receives no net of tax income from the asset and each year tax cuts into its capital value until at length the capital sum all goes in tax. The only advantage he has got from the legacy is that it has postponed the rate of decline in his wealth. This may seem a very small advantage to offset against the alternative course of action of spending the £2,000 on consumption — say a holiday spree abroad or a party to celebrate Aunt Jemima's generosity.

2. *A threat to the growing points of new enterprise by its effects on the closely owned business.* Although we are considering a personal wealth tax, it will affect businesses which are owned by one or a small number of persons whose wealth consists predominantly of business assets.

An additive wealth tax can cause problems in a number of ways:
(a) In the initial stages of a potentially profitable business, wealth tax has to be paid on the value of business assets even though no profits have been gained; establishing a new enterprise is thus made more difficult.
(b) An established business may run into a loss-making period because, say, a vital export market is closed to its products by political action. It then needs to develop new markets and perhaps diversify its products. At this difficult time, payment of wealth tax has to continue.
(c) In the most general terms, it is clear that the expansion of a business is likely to be restricted if the combined income tax and wealth tax bill of the owners exceeds their income — or what is left of their income after allowance for their reasonable consumption requirements. Indeed, the problem is recognised in the Green Paper. The Green Paper rejects the solution of exempting business assets or farms or of calculating liabilities on such assets on specially favourable terms. It suggests that a ceiling might be of considerable help to businessmen and farmers and continues:

> Where a taxpayer had no assets out of which he could reasonably pay
> the wealth tax he might also be allowed to defer payment of the tax
> attributable to productive assets, subject to interest (which might also be
> deferred) at a commercial rate, until the owner sells the assets, retires or
> dies — any provision for deferment on these lines would be extended as
> far as appropriate to cover shares in unquoted trading companies. This
> would ensure that the founder of a business, or the entrepreneur who
> built it up, would not himself have to pay the tax while he was running it.

We shall say a little about the special problems of agriculture in a
moment. But let us follow out some of the implications of the
proposal to allow deferment on these terms.

The effect of the deferment provision on a business depends on
certain crucial and inter-related factors — in particular the rate of
interest, the general rate of inflation, the changes in the value of
business assets, the rates of wealth tax and threshold and any
adjustments therein over time. But it can be shown that on certain
not implausible assumptions, a business or farm could be rendered
bankrupt by the deferment of charge 'at a commercial rate' of
interest.

Examples are all of a business or farm of which the net value is
£880,000. Non-business assets are assumed to be exactly equal to
personal debts. Interest is assumed to be charged at 9% compound.
(For income tax purposes simple interest is used, but for longer
time periods we assume compound interest would be applied.)
Such a rate is well below the current market rate of interest.
Accumulated wealth tax debt and interest is deducted each year
before arriving at the wealth tax charge for that year.

(i) If in these circumstances the gross value of business assets
remained constant, at wealth tax scale B of the Green Paper the
estate would be *bankrupt after 24 years.*

(ii) If the value of business assets were falling at 5% per annum,
on wealth tax scale B the estate would be *bankrupt after 19
years.*

(iii) If the value of business assets remained constant for *16
years* and then suddenly halved, on wealth tax scale B the
business would *immediately fall into bankruptcy.*

It may be argued that these examples are misleading; that if
there were no inflation, then the interest rate which would be
employed would be much less than 9%, whilst if inflation justified
a 9% interest rate the value of business assets would be rising.
Whilst it can be readily accepted that, if conditions were stable,
we might expect this kind of constant relationship, such is not

current experience. Asset prices have moved in the opposite direction to the general price level; currently, for example, we have a 20-30% rate of general inflation but land prices are stable or falling (and the introduction of a wealth tax can be expected to accentuate a fall which may be prolonged). And we have seen stock exchange prices varying between very wide limits during the past three years. Whilst the examples we have set out of estates becoming bankrupt as a result of wealth tax may not describe typical effects, they are nonetheless realistic possibilities.

Moreover, although there may be very few instances in which firms are actually rendered bankrupt as a result of wealth tax, the burden of a deferred debt, constituting a substantial proportion of business or farm assets, will be commonplace if a wealth tax is introduced on the lines of the illustrative scales in the Green Paper and without significant reduction in rates of income tax. It can be readily agreed that there are circumstances in which a debt can be a spur to endeavour; but this occurs where the debtor can see some possibility of eliminating the debt by his own efforts. The wealth tax debt is not of this kind and must surely have an adverse effect on the rationality of decision-taking and on risk bearing.

3. *At best a difficult transition period for agriculture; at worst the impairment of its efficiency through a reduction of investment and the fragmentation of farms.*

The big rise in agricultural land prices since the war and especially in the early 1970's has brought many owner-occupiers as well as large agricultural landlords within the scope of the wealth tax. An additive wealth tax carries the danger that landlords, in order to pay the tax, will cut back on investment and perhaps sell parcels of land. If complete farms are sold no ill economic consequences need ensue. Also if smaller parcels of land are sold there need be no damage to agricultural efficiency if they are bought to be added to existing farms — but, with a wealth tax and CTT in operation, buyers may be scarce.

Perhaps the most danger of economic damage lies in the effect on owner-occupiers, who now constitute the predominant form of landowner. Unlike the large landowner they have not got the option of selling off a farm and still remaining in agriculture. The temptation for them to reduce investment or sell small parcels of land must be acute unless special concessions are granted — though the Green Paper says that the Government has set its face against such concessions other than the possibility of deferment. The possible consequences of deferment we have already considered.

One crucial factor in determining the effects of an additive wealth tax on agriculture is the movement in the price of land. Land is a stock, about one and a half percent of which currently comes on the market in a year. Because land is more or less fixed in extent, its value can undergo big changes within a short space of time. The combined effect of Capital Transfer Tax and Wealth Tax may well be to bring more land annually onto the market whilst at the same time reducing the number of buyers. This will undoubtedly depress the price of land below what it would otherwise have been. Whether it will fall in money terms or in real terms compared with other assets, depends on which other factors are at work — in particular, how far land continues to be purchased as a hedge against galloping inflation.

A substantial fall in land prices could well be to the long term benefit of the agricultural industry and would also serve to take many owner-occupiers out of the wealth tax range. But a sudden price decline could hardly fail to generate a crop of bankruptcies — of those who had bought on borrowed money at the inflated prices of the early seventies.

4. *An additive wealth tax could hardly fail to act as a stimulus to avoidance, including the emigration of the rich with their wealth.* Perhaps more serious, it would encourage the emigration of enterprising persons who had not yet reached the wealth tax threshold, but saw themselves as potentially rich.

In short, an additive wealth tax could have some immediate effect on inequality by reducing, annually, the wealth of the rich; but, especially if introduced at a time of low business confidence, growing unemployment and strong inflation, a wealth tax of this kind could undermine private enterprise and completely upset the balance of the mixed economy.

This is not to argue against an annual wealth tax which was a substitute for, rather than added to, existing rates of income tax. Such a substitutive wealth tax, which the wealthy would be able to pay (along with income tax) from income, has many attractions. But such a tax would mainly serve other policy objectives than a reduction in inequality of wealth. It would only assist to reduce wealth inequality in so far as it taxed more heavily wealthy persons who had previously avoided progressive income tax by holding nil-yielding or low-yielding assets.

Objectives of Policy

This analysis raises various issues which require a more careful
definition of policy objectives. Let us consider some of them.

First, is the possession of large wealth to be regarded as a sin
irrespective of how it was derived, or is the source of the wealth
important? Should wealth acquired by enterprise and saving be
taxed equally with wealth derived from inheritance, capital gains
or winning the football pools? Take two men, identical in terms
of family circumstances, both earning the same, high, life-time
incomes. One spends all his income on consumption; the other
lives frugally, saves and reinvests the income from his saving. A
wealth tax will hit the second, not the first — but has the saver
been more anti-social than the spender?

In this argument about source of wealth it is relevant to recall
that Professor Harbury's researches, the subject of an earlier paper,
point strongly to inheritance as the most important cause of
inequality in the distribution of wealth.

If all wealth is to be regarded as equally reprehensible, then a
wealth tax is an obvious instrument to use to reduce wealth
inequalities. If a more discriminating approach is sought, by which
wealth is taxed differently according to its source, then the policy
should rest primarily on wealth transfer taxes — death duties, gift
taxes, capital gains taxes.

A related point is that the case for reducing inequality of wealth
is sometimes presented, by the present Chancellor amongst others,
as a way of improving the social climate, of getting a fairer society,
in which people will be more prepared to accept personal sacrifices
in the common interest; e.g. that an incomes policy will be more
acceptable to wage-earners if wealth inequalities are being eliminated. This is a proposition that has never really been tested. In
particular, if inequalities of wealth are resented, is the resentment
a blanket one, or does resentment relate to wealth obtained in
particular 'easy' ways by inheritance or fortuitous capital gains?
Again, is resentment related to the way wealth is used? Is it
conspicuous consumption rather than the possession of wealth
which generates resentment? *This is a load of crap!*

It is possible that an additive wealth tax could be counter-
productive of the social cohesion that is one of its underlying
objectives. As we have seen, a likely outcome of an additive wealth
tax is dis-saving and increased consumption by the rich. The visible
signs of wealth might then add to social bitterness, especially if the

increased share of current output which the rich were appropriating came at a time of national austerity and unemployment. The contrast can be painted in an extreme form. A large farmer, who owns his farm, may be worth half a million pounds, his assets consisting almost entirely of land which he has no intention of selling. He works hard and lives frugally. An additive wealth tax might lead such a man, in frustration and desperation, to sell his land, abandon independent farming and adopt a much more extravagant life-style. Before the wealth tax his wealth might not have been an object of resentment; afterwards it may become so.

A further vital issue of policy is the importance of speed in the reduction in inequality of wealth. What price are we prepared to pay for its achievement? A heavy additive annual wealth tax could bring some rapid results but at serious economic cost. There is a vital difference between the economic consequences of death duties and of a heavy additive wealth tax. Death duties do not hit the creators of new businesses and their economic effects are not necessarily detrimental. A heavy additive wealth tax, imposed without major relief for productive assets, would hit the growth point of new enterprise.

The ultimate question concerns the sort of society we want. If we seek a socialist society with the means of production and the vast majority of wealth owned by the state, then a CTT, which promotes equality entirely by the transfer of assets to the state, and a heavy additive wealth tax, with no concessions to private businesses, is a logical policy if we are prepared to accept the costs of transition. On the other hand, if we seek to reduce inequality within a mixed economy, with a large private enterprise sector, then an AT, which operates partly by encouraging a wider diffusion of wealth within the private sector, is to be preferred to a CTT; and an additive wealth tax is inappropriate as a main instrument for reducing inequality.

A number of alternative combinations of taxes on wealth are possible, of which we have only been able to consider some. We have said little about capital gains taxes and nothing at all about another possibility — a once and for all capital levy; but, if reducing inequality rapidly is an over-riding consideration, a capital levy might do so with less long-term economic harm than a continuing additive wealth tax. These alternative wealth tax combinations differ in their effectiveness to reduce inequality, in the philosophy of wealth which they embody, in the economic costs and benefits which they generate, and in the ultimate form

of society to which they lead. As citizens in a democracy we have
a right to expect our political leaders, who push through policies
on the taxation of wealth, to weigh up these matters and tell us the
outcome plainly. Unfortunately, there is little indication that the
effects of alternative policies on inequality have been carefully
considered. The Select Committee on Wealth Tax has recently
been taking evidence from members of the Board of Inland
Revenue. Mr John Pardoe MP, having indicated some of the possible alternatives, put the question to Mr W. H. B. Johnson: 'Has
the Board of Inland Revenue ever done a study to show which of
these methods would achieve the fairer distribution of wealth that
is apparently desired?' Reply: 'Not a study in that sense. These are
questions which are always under examination, of course. You
cannot study the effects of a particular tax until you have it.'

Mr Pardoe repeated the point, with a particular reference to the
alternative effects of a gift tax on the donor or the donee, and put
the specific question: 'Have you actually been asked for this
study?' — Answer: 'Not a formal study, no.'[8]

If no formal studies have been asked for by government of the
alternative means of achieving a reduction in inequality, still less
does any coherent philosophy of wealth seem to have been
formulated. It is a sad reflection on the process of policy-making
that *after* the Labour Government had committed itself to a
capital transfer tax and a wealth tax to reduce inequalities in the
distribution of wealth it should *then* set up a Royal Commission
to produce information about the distribution of income and
wealth.

Perhaps, in conclusion, I should come clean about my own
philosophy. I want to see a reduction in inequality of wealth
within the context of a mixed economy by means of policies
which include the taxation of wealth. For this purpose I favour
wealth transfer taxes, which tax wealth differently according to
its source; the keystone of my policy would be the taxation of
inheritance by means of an accessions tax together with a heavier,
but indexed, capital gains tax. My guess is that a majority of the
population and indeed of the government share my objective of
a reduction in inequality of wealth within a mixed economy. My
fear is that the objective may not be attained, and that the mixed
economy itself may be undermined, not because of a determined
design to establish a socialist state, but through muddle-headed-
ness or the myopic pursuit of short-term political advantage, or
both.

Notes and references

1 Nicholas Kaldor, 'The reform of personal taxation', *Essays in Economic Policy*, Duckworth 1964, vol. 1, pp 212-13.
2 C. T. Sandford, J. R. M. Willis and D. J. Ironside, *An Accessions Tax*, Institute for Fiscal Studies 1973, especially chs 10, 11, 12.
3 Robin Barlow *et al.*, *Economic Behaviour of the Affluent*, The Brookings Institution 1966, pp 31-33.
4 E. R. Rolph and G. F. Break, *Public Finance*, The Ronald Press Company, New York, 1961, p 266.
5 Jonathan Boswell, *The Rise and Decline of Small Firms*, Allen & Unwin 1972.
6 *Report of the Committee of Inquiry on Small Firms*, Cmnd 4811, November 1971, p 225.
7 The marginal rate of income tax may be defined as the tax that would be paid on an additional £100 of investment income; the marginal rate of wealth tax is the tax that would be paid on that amount of additional wealth required to generate an additional £100 of income.
8 Select Committee on Wealth Tax, *Minutes of Evidence*, 29 January 1975, p 11.

8 Trade unions and social equality

In their *History of Trade Unionism* Sidney and Beatrice Webb
defined a trade union as a 'continuous association of wage-
earners for the purpose of maintaining or improving the conditions
of their working lives'.

Up to 1824 it was the policy of the state to prohibit agreements
for the regulation of wages or of other conditions of employment,
on the grounds that the rights and duties of everyone were laid
down and guaranteed by the laws and customs of the country.
Since the end was offensive, so were the means, and workpeople
were forbidden by law to combine for the purpose of raising wages.
A trade union as defined by the Webbs — and even a temporary
association for the same purpose — was, therefore, a combination
to do an unlawful act; a criminal conspiracy.

The Acts against combinations were repealed in 1824. Since
then no class of wage or salary earner has been hindered by law
from forming a trade union or from defining its more particular
objects or the limits and qualifications of its membership or its
internal structure and administration. Rather to the contrary,
successive governments in the nineteenth and the first half of this
century have, for the most part, been willing to remove by statute
the taint of common law illegality which the courts after 1824 had
continued to attach to certain acts done in combination and in
furtherance of a trade dispute.

However, in the same period, governments have also shown an
equivalent reluctance positively to endow trade unions with legal
122

rights as distinct from or in addition to allowing them certain legal immunities. In matters concerning terms and conditions of employment, a trade union cannot use a court of law to require its members to observe its rules or instructions or an employer to make and to observe any agreement – even though such rules, instructions and agreements have been lawfully made for lawful purposes. The kind of agreements among workpeople and between workpeople and employers which were prohibited by statute up to 1824 are now lawful but they are not legally enforceable. For more than a hundred years the state aspired to an attitude of neutrality and non-intervention in industrial relations – an attitude which permitted, but did not encourage, governments to provide limited legal safeguards for particular purposes, such as minimum standards of safety and health at work and payments during unemployment and sickness; or for some special classes of workpeople such as limiting the hours of work of women and young persons and fixing minimum wages for badly paid workpeople in unorganised trades.

The safeguards provided by such measures were deliberately meagre in order not to provoke complaints from employers of undue discrimination or to discourage workpeople from trying to get better protection through trade unionism. They reflect the limited extent to which governments in the 19th and the first half of the 20th century were prepared to go to bring some relief to the most oppressed categories of working people. Generally, all the issues between all workpeople and their employers were left to be settled by mutual agreement without the interference of the law either in the making of an agreement or its enforcement. Trade unions were and still are entirely lawful bodies most of whose activities are, nevertheless, carried on outside the reach of the law.

This has often been described and criticised as a position of legal privilege. In fact it was in its origins no more than a necessary consequence of the reluctance of the state to accept any responsibility for safeguarding the interests of people at work. That responsibility was left entirely to workpeople themselves. If, therefore, the state was unwilling or incapable of protecting workpeople against low pay and poor working conditions, governments could not, at the same time, prohibit workpeople from forming their own organisations for that purpose or maintain laws which imposed serious limitations on the ability of those organisations to fulfil that purpose.

The attitude of indifference of governments has now changed. All postwar governments have shown by their actions that they are not content to leave the state with a negligible and largely impassive role in industrial relations. For example:

(a) Modern legal safeguards, available to all workpeople, give substantial protection against abrupt or unfair dismissal, compensation for loss of employment and the right, in some circumstances, to require an employer to include the terms of a collective agreement in the individual contracts of his workpeople.

(b) The Industrial Relations Act of 1971 contained provisions by which an employer could be required to recognise a particular trade union as the proper body exclusively to represent some grades or classes of his workpeople; to provide facilities in an undertaking for trade union representatives to carry out their trade union duties; and to supply trade unions with information about the finances, the plans and the prospects of a company and its undertakings. The 1971 Act was repealed in 1974 but not because the then Parliament thought that these particular provisions were offensive. Indeed, similar provisions will be included in a Bill shortly to be introduced to the present Parliament with, probably, a further obligation on employers to reserve seats on a Board of Management for persons appointed by trade unions or elected by trade unionists.

(c) In 1969 a Labour Government issued a White Paper, *In Place of Strife*, which proposed that a Minister of Labour should have the power, under penalty, to order workpeople and trade unions to delay industrial action for a period of up to 28 days during which the parties would be expected to try to reach a settlement by negotiation; to order a trade union to hold a ballot of its members before calling a strike; and to order a union to accept a decision of the Trades Union Congress on a dispute with another union about trade union membership. The 1971 Industrial Relations Act passed by a Conservative Government, enabled a specially constituted Industrial Court to order 'cooling off' periods and strike ballots; to determine issues concerning trade union membership, trade union recognition and collective bargaining procedures; and prohibited or imposed conditions limiting the use of industrial action for these and for some other purposes specified in the Act.

(d) Every government since the end of the Second World War
has tried to induce or to compel the parties to collective agreements to restrain wage and salary increases in accordance with
official criteria or within limits defined by the government with
the agreement or despite the objections of one or other of the
two sides of industry.

There have been White Papers and Ministerial pronouncements;
a Declaration of Intent and a Social Contract; all urging wage
restraint as a national necessity. Governments have tried to
reinforce general exhortations to conform to national incomes
policy by giving direct guidance or instructions to the boards of
nationalised industries and to statutory wage-fixing bodies and
by appointing (successively) a commission, a council and a
board to scrutinise and to comment on wage claims and wage
settlements in the light of government policy. There have been
two Acts of Parliament enabling a Minister to impose, under
penalties, some specific restrictions on wage negotiations and
wage settlements — the early warning and standstill provisions
of the Prices and Incomes Act of 1966 and the provisions
relating to permissible wage increases of the Counter Inflation
Act of 1973.

Have these various measures and efforts of post-war governments any significance except to illustrate the obvious fact that
modern governments are under greater political pressure than
their predecessors to promote the welfare of the poorer sections
of the community?

The additional legal safeguards for workpeople — mentioned
in (a) — can perhaps be explained or explained away as not
essentially different from the measures used even in the 19th
century to give special relief in cases of hardship. In fact, only
the means are the same. The recent measures give far more
extensive and generous statutory protection than would ever
have been contemplated by a pre-war government. They are,
therefore, better to be compared and associated with the kind of
public services provided under the name of the 'welfare state'.
In common with the services of the welfare state they have the
aim and the effects of making a positive and substantial contribution towards maintaining and improving the conditions of
life for working people. The difference is simply that the benefits
of the welfare state are extended to workpeople as citizens.

In the early part of this century many trade unionists believed that the establishment of boards to fix statutory minimum wages in certain trades would hinder the growth of trade unionism and collective agreements in those trades. For the same reason, the Trades Union Congress remained opposed to State Family Allowances up to the outbreak of the Second World War.

Yet the trade unions do not see any challenge to trade unionism in these more recent efforts to improve the conditions of life for working people. On the contrary, the Trades Union Congress had discussed with every government since 1962 the possibilities of reaching an agreement or an understanding by which the govern- ment, on its part, would undertake to extend and improve the social services and the TUC, on its part, would advise trade unions to conform to nationally agreed policies on wage increases.

It would be unsafe, as yet, to make assumptions about the willingness of the parties to continue these particular discussions or their ability to sustain any understanding they may reach. The 'Declaration of Intent' of 1965 was an understanding between the government, the TUC and the Confederation of British Industry which, after only six months, the government decided needed to be reinforced by legislation. There were intensive discussions between the government, the TUC and the CBI during 1972 which did not lead to any common understanding and the government went on with legislation to which the TUC was opposed. On the other hand, the present 'social contract' is based on an understanding reached in discussions between the TUC and the Labour Opposition in 1973, and the TUC and the CBI discussed with, and announced that they generally agreed with, the proposals of the White Paper, *The Attack on Inflation,* issued in July of this year.

Even if it is eventually seen that none of these discussions have produced anything that came to very much in practice or that they have all led to results very different from what was intended, they do, nevertheless, serve to show that there is nowadays a large measure of agreement among governments and the two central bodies most representative of trade unions and of employers that:

the state has an important role to play alongside the trade unions in maintaining or improving the conditions of life for working people; and that

on that basis, a government has a corresponding right to a view about the conduct of wage negotiations and wage settlements.

That could not have been said of any period between 1824 and 1940. Indeed, in the matter of ends, a modern government is

closer to a government of the last quarter of the 18th century than
to a government in the last quarter of the 19th century. The main
impediments to government action in recent years have been
differences and uncertainties about the proper means.

The proposals — mentioned in (b) above — to require employers
to give facilities to trade unions and trade union representatives to
carry out their work may be described as simply for the purpose
of improving the capacity of trade unions to reach agreements
with employers acceptable to both parties without altering the
voluntary nature of trade unionism or of collective agreements.
In that respect, these proposals are intended to serve the same
purpose that 19th century governments had in mind in removing
the legal restrictions on certain acts done in combination or in
furtherance of a trade dispute and in making available at public
expense services for conciliation and arbitration in industrial
disputes.

However, if the object is much the same, the means are significantly different. Nineteenth and early 20th century governments
acted to *remove* common law restraints which were inhibiting
the actions of workpeople and trade unions; these measures will
impose statutory obligations on employers. Moreover, they are
only the residue of a series of proposals and measures — including
those mentioned in (c) above — directed towards improving
collective bargaining by enlarging the role of the state in industrial
relations.

Looking at the large and growing number of industrial disputes
and, more particularly, at the kind of issues involved and at the
number of instances of forms of industrial action other than a
straightforward official strike, governments have been convinced
that many disputes arise from the weaknesses of an almost entirely
voluntary system of industrial relations — from the lack of enthusiasm for trade unionism of some employers and managements and
the limited view of all managements of the scope of the matters
proper to be jointly negotiated, and from the inability or the
unwillingness of trade unions to direct their members to raise and
pursue their claims and grievances through the established
procedures.

The proposals of the White Paper, *In Place of Strife*, in 1969 and
the provisions of the Industrial Relations Act of 1971 aimed at
providing remedies for these weaknesses. Though the details were
very different the intention in both cases was to bring pressure to
bear on reluctant managements to recognise and to negotiate with

trade unions and on delinquent workpeople and trade unions to follow established practices and procedures. The White Paper and the Act were, in fact, attempts by governments to allow the state to play a larger part in defining and, where necessary, enforcing standards of good industrial conduct.

These particular attempts were largely frustrated. The trade unions strongly objected to the proposals to enable legal sanctions to be used against trade unions and workpeople as impracticable and an altogether unjustifiable invasion of the voluntary principle. The TUC persuaded the government to drop these proposals from the White Paper. Nevertheless, the government managed to assert its right to be concerned about industrial relations by getting in return from the TUC a 'solemn and binding' undertaking that the TUC itself would take prompt and direct action to deal with unofficial strikes and inter-union disputes.

The CBI agreed to the legal obligations imposed on employers by the 1971 Industrial Relations Act but only because the Act also imposed obligations on trade unions and workpeople. The trade unions used all the means legally open to them to make the Act ineffective and it was repealed in 1974. However, the Trade Unions and Labour Relations Act of 1974 re-enacted the provisions of the 1971 Act which made it 'the duty of the Secretary of State to maintain a code of practice . . . for the purpose of promoting good industrial relations'.

The Secretary of State is also required to consult the TUC and the CBI when drafting or revising a code of practice. However, like the Highway Code, its provisions will not be directly enforceable in the courts.

A code of practice is, therefore, intended to be of the nature of an understanding or a voluntary agreement between the government, representing the public interest; the TUC representing the interests of workpeople; and the CBI representing the interests of employers, about the proper conduct of relations within companies and workshops. In that respect it is similar to the 'social contract' which sets out the considerations that negotiators are expected to take into account in wage settlements.

The code of practice is, so far, the only means of enabling a government to bring its influence to bear in the field of industrial relations which is acceptable in principle to each of the main political parties, to the TUC and to the CBI. The TUC is opposed to any measures which would allow legal sanctions to be imposed on workpeople or on trade unions. The CBI objects to an extension of the legal obligations of employers to workpeople unaccompanied by corresponding legal obligations on trade unions and workpeople. Governments for their part, though usually willing to discuss their proposals with representatives of the interests likely to be affected, normally prefer to derive their authority exclusively from Parliament and to be able to act with the certainty provided by legislation.

The present government has, for the time being at any rate, decided that any attempt to impose additional legal obligations or restrictions on workpeople or trade unions would have the practical effect of diminishing rather than increasing its ability to influence the conduct of industrial relations.

Legislation, involving penalties for default, will be used for some special purposes such as to require employers to recognise trade unions, to disclose information to their workpeople and to reserve seats on a Supervisory Board of a company for trade unionists. Apart from such special purposes (for most of which some future government will, in any case, have to legislate as a consequence of the United Kingdom's membership of the European Economic Community) the present government hopes to be able to play a sufficiently effective part in the development of industrial relations generally, and in wage settlements in particular, by means of discussion and agreement with the central bodies representing the two sides of industry and without resort to legal compulsion.

These means are, clearly, more closely in accord with the views and attitudes of the trade unions than of employers. That could have been expected in any case of a Labour Government, and the CBI and employers generally will certainly hope to persuade this or a future government to make some changes in the detailed provisions of the code of practice and the terms of the social contract. Nevertheless, this method of discussion and agreement with both sides of industry on ends and means is also clearly based on conclusions drawn from experience of the failures of two recent governments to define and to enforce standards of good conduct in industrial relations by law. It was the opposition of the trade unions, not of the employers, which caused a Labour Government to withdraw the penal provisions of the White Paper, *In Place of Strife*, in 1969 and which made ineffective the 1971 Industrial Relations Act and the 1973 Counter Inflation Act of a Conservative Government.

The possibility that a government may be able to persuade the trade unions to modify their opposition to legal constraints on workpeople is too remote to be considered. In the circumstances, no government will readily discard the alternative possibilities of determining the main objective and the means of its industrial relations policies by a process of discussion and substantial agreement with the CBI and, particularly, the TUC. The uncertainties surrounding future developments in relations between the trade unions and governments are as to whether the parties, and especially governments, will remain satisfied with the practical results of these largely voluntary arrangements.

In the original *Social Contract* Rousseau said that he was dealing with the change that came about by which 'man is born free; and everywhere he is in chains'. The present social contract and the other efforts and activities of post-war governments already described raise a similar question, namely, how has it come about that after more than a century during which governments and trade unions operated largely at arms length from each other, they are now earnestly trying to find purposes and means by which they can cooperate.

The unions have always had some political objectives which they considered were quite consistent with their objections to any legal supervision or regulation of their own purposes and practices. The Webbs first described the purpose of a trade union as 'maintaining or improving conditions of employment.' They later substituted the words 'the conditions of the working lives' of their members. The Webbs made this change to exclude the implication that trade unions have always contemplated the continuance of 'a capitalist or wage system'.

In fact, some of the largest unions affiliated to the TUC are neutral on this question and no trade union in the United Kingdom requires a member to support or to oppose any political party. The change was, however, justified for the reasons that trade unions generally have always been concerned with the welfare of working people as a class and have never supposed that they could properly safeguard the industrial interests of their members solely by the method of collective bargaining with employers — even in those instances in which the employer is the state. The trade unions have always expected the state to provide at least a minimum of protection for workpeople against miserably low wages, injury and excessive hours of labour as well as public services for the relief of the aged, the sick and the unemployed.

They were, however, slow in developing a distinctive political attitude and in formulating anything that could be described as a programme of legislative demands and it was not until 1868 that a number of trade unions decided to establish a central body — the Trades Union Congress — 'for the purpose of bringing the trades into closer alliance and to take action in all Parliamentary matters pertaining to the general interests of the working classes'.

From then on the trade unions became increasingly concerned to supplement their industrial activities and objectives by political action and objectives.

In its early years, the efforts of the TUC were mainly directed towards pressing parliaments and governments to deal with outstanding social problems of particular concern to workpeople and their families — education and public health and protection against or relief for unemployment, injury, gross exploitation and old-age.

Even in those days the trade unions were often criticised for misusing their power and exceeding their proper functions. The same criticism is more widespread and acute in these days when trade unions are more powerful; have enlarged their political objectives; and nowadays seek to and, in fact, succeed in influencing or frustrating the economic, industrial and financial, as well as the social, policies of a government.

To the trade unions, however, it is as necessary to their original and essential purposes that they should be able to influence national economic and industrial policies as it is for them to be able to bargain with the employers of their members about wages and working conditions. Trade unions have learned from experience that their efforts within industry to improve the conditions of the lives of working people can be frustrated by the action which governments take or fail to take in managing the economy and in maintaining or developing public services. It is very much in the trade unions' own interest and, therefore, an important part of their purpose, to establish and maintain an effective working relationship with a government. That, indeed, is the reason why the trade unions helped to create the Labour Party.

Up to the Second World War, governments of other parties looked upon the trade unions rather as a means, or as an excuse, for a government not having itself to become deeply involved in industrial affairs. Many of the policies supported and urged upon governments by the trade unions involve a degree of state intervention in economic and industrial questions which most pre-war governments considered quite impracticable as well as undesirable.

The really significant post-war change — the change which has compelled modern governments to concern themselves with and to attempt to influence or to regulate trade union practices and the conduct of industrial relations generally — is described in the opening words of a White Paper, *Employment Policy after the War,* published in 1944 by the war-time Coalition Government of the three political parties. These are 'the government accepts as its primary aim and responsibility the maintenance of a high and stable level of employment after the war'. Some post-war governments have shown less enthusiasm than others for this commitment and the political parties have different views about the particular measures best suited to maintain a high level of employment. But no post-war government as yet has repudiated the commitment or the consequential responsibilities of a modern government for industrial efficiency, the supply, use and training of manpower, for the balance of trade and payments, etc and, perhaps most important of all, for industrial costs, prices and incomes. Governments, as well as trade unions, learn from experience and post-war governments have learned that their efforts in these fields can be frustrated by the actions or inactions of employers and of trade unions.

There are therefore reasons, important to the government, to employers and to the trade unions, which make it desirable for these three parties to reach a common understanding, not simply on generalisations about the ends they seek but also about the practical means by which they can be reached. In a democracy no one of these parties alone has control over all of these means, though each has the power to frustrate the effects of the others.

Neither the employers nor the trade unions could or would be willing to hand over their responsibilities or their powers to the state and compulsion has been shown to be impracticable. The most likely alternative to cooperation is that governments will have to modify or abandon their commitment to maintain a high level of employment and their consequential responsibilities for economic growth, stable prices and good industrial relations. If that should happen and if, in consequence, this country were to return to the industrial instability and the heavy unemployment of pre-war days, that would certainly not improve the ability of the trade unions collectively to secure greater social justice and fairness for their members. And, despite the idiosyncracies of some individual unions and the uncertainties that must still be attached to the possibilities that trade unions, with their unique and special responsibilities to particular groups of workpeople, will be able to remain for long in agreement with any government about wages, it is surely still too early to say that they will not want or may not be able to pursue their aim of 'maintaining or improving the conditions of the working lives' of their members by a process of negotiation and voluntary agreement with governments as well as employers.

PAUL GROUT
University of Manchester

9 Rawlsian justice and economic theory

Introduction

Rawls's book, *A Theory of Justice*[1] is the most interesting contribution to moral philosophy for decades and even though it was only published in 1972 it has already started to influence the field of welfare economics. The aim of this paper is to show the relationship of moral philosophy to basic welfare economics and to give an insight into the economic implications of the adoption of Rawls's principles of justice.

Basic Welfare Economics

The most basic and least disputed value judgment in welfare economics is the belief that any acceptable distribution must satisfy the criterion of Pareto efficiency. A distribution is Pareto efficient if it is impossible to make any individual better off without making at least one individual worse off in the process. To understand the relationship between Pareto efficiency and economic theory, we need to discuss briefly the most basic structure of economic theory, that of a competitive equilibrium (for a classic treatment see ref. 2). The aim of this basic structure is to represent in a simple form an economy where all individuals and firms are acting competitively, i.e. no one individual or firm acting alone can influence prices.

In the simple model we assume all individuals have convex

134

preferences (their indifference curves are of the simple textbook type) and that production sets are convex (constant and increasing returns to scale are ruled out). With the addition of further weak assumptions we can use a fixed point theorem to prove that in all cases where firms and individuals are competitive, and satisfy these assumptions, prices for goods and labour will exist such that there will be no excess supply or demand in any market, i.e. a competititve equilibrium will exist.

We can go further than this and prove a theorem which tells us that a competitive equilibrium will be Pareto efficient.[3] The theorem either in this form or its converse is frequently referred to as the fundamental theorem of welfare economics. While this forms a strong base for welfare economics the economist must go further if he wishes to say anything about unique distributions.

Since the concept of Pareto efficiency stands relatively unchallenged in welfare economics one would not be surprised to find that generally the set of Pareto efficient distributions has infinite members. Consider the simple case where, on a desert island, a fixed amount of food is available to distribute between two individuals whose utility depends on their own consumption alone. Any splitting of the food into two sections will be a Pareto efficient allocation including the distribution which leaves one individual to starve while the other consumes all the food available on the island. So, clearly, while the fundamental theorem of welfare economics is important, we need to go much further if we are to say anything to help society choose an optimal distribution of resources.

Once one leaves the comparative acceptability of Pareto efficiency and starts to rank Pareto efficient points, then obtaining widespread support for particular value judgments becomes less common. There appear to be three main paths to follow from this point. One is to view the whole process of ranking Pareto efficient points as being outside the realm of economics and hence reject welfare economics as a valid subject. The strongest advocate of this approach is Graaff whose book, *Theoretical Welfare Economics*,[4] as Baumol[5] so aptly put it, bore 'an ill-concealed resemblance to obituary notices.' A second approach is to choose conditions that we feel must be satisfied by any method of ranking possible distributions, and then see whether any ranking processes exist which satisfy these conditions. The initiative in this area came from Arrow in his classic book on social choice,[6] but has since tended, with a few notable exceptions, to be rather negative in its approach. For this reason the third approach is separate from the previous one, the third being to look to moral philosophy for the alternative concepts of justice, use economic theory to determine their economic implications and to choose an acceptable method of ranking distributions from the alternatives. The rest of this paper will look in detail at the economic implications of Rawls's approach to moral philosophy and compare it to the most historically entrenched of all the concepts of justice — utilitarianism.

Rawlsian Justice

The utilitarian philosophy is based on the initially appealing view that the aim of society is to create the greatest happiness for the greatest number. In economic terms this means society's institutions should be manipulated to maximise the sum of the individuals' utilities in society. While this view has dominated thinking on moral philosophy for centuries, it has increasingly come under criticism in recent years. The economists' criticism was initially against the use of utilitarian philosophy since it introduced normative aspects to a subject many economists believed should be a pure science. However, in the last decade most of the criticism of utilitarian philosophy has not come from this direction. Many economists realise the necessary relationship between moral philosophy and welfare economics and criticise utilitarian philosophy not because of its normative aspects but because of its implications for the distribution of resources. A classic example given against the utilitarian philosophy is the following. If an individual is, say, a cripple and hence cannot get as much pleasure from his allocation as a healthy individual, under a utilitarian distribution he will get less than a normal individual, whereas many people instinctively feel that society should try to compensate these individuals for their unfortunate incapacity. To take the recent example of thalidomide children, can society find acceptable a view of moral philosophy which not only would fail to agree with compensating these children but would actually allocate these children less resources than the average healthy child? These are the aspects of utilitarian philosophy that Rawls finds unacceptable and led him to produce his counter view of justice which he has spelt out in detail.[1]

Rawls believes that society cannot agree on what constitutes a just allocation of income, wealth and power because the decision process takes place when individuals are in possession of morally irrelevant information. Clearly, a man who has a million pounds and a penniless tramp will not agree on what is a fair amount of wealth tax for an individual to pay and the difference in their relative wealth is almost certain to enter their decision process. However, if individuals are attempting to define principles they consider to be morally just then their own position in society should not affect their view. Thus Rawls argues that true princi- ✳ ples of justice will be the ones that individuals would choose if they did not know what chance they had of being rich, what chance they had of being intelligent, healthy, etc. He uses most of the book to argue that individuals would be afraid of being born very poor and thus, in complete contrast to the utilitarian philosophy, they would choose to maximise the welfare of the worst off in society, i.e. they would choose the maximin concept of justice (for a full account of the principles Rawls feels indivi- duals would choose see p 302 of his book).

It is essential to Rawls's analyses that the individuals are unsure of their chance of being in any particular position in society since it has been shown by Harsanyi[7] that if individuals believe they have an equal chance of being in any position in society then they will choose the utilitarian philosophy. Thus whether individuals believe the choice of just principles comes better from one type of uncertainty rather than another becomes important. I do not wish to discuss the debate on the logical consistency of Rawls's derivation as compared to Harsanyi's, save to add to it that in choosing the equal probability case in preference to the unknown probability case individuals may fail to satisfy one of Harsanyi's necessary assumptions, and that in accepting Rawls's stance the individual may be accepting one of Harsanyi's strongest assump- tions (see Appendix A).

However, this does not reduce Rawls's contribution to moral philosophy, while the maximin principle will be accepted or rejected by the economist on its implications for the economic system. We now turn to the implications of maximin in three areas — income tax, education and economic growth — and compare in each case the outcomes with the utilitarian equivalents.

Income Tax

In economic theory the main method of redistributing economic

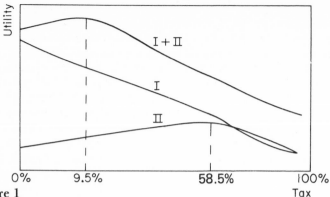

Figure 1

resources is through income tax since the assets which affect an
individual's ability to earn income, e.g. mental ability, strength,
education, cannot be transferred to another individual, i.e. lump-
sum taxes are infeasible. Since the individual owns the assets, he
can choose how intensively he utilises them; hence this always
places a restriction on how much income tax can be levied on an
individual. If we wish to redistribute the income of someone with
high earning ability, placing a 100% tax on his income will not
aid the poor since he will simply stop working. Suppose we have
an individual who can choose how many hours he works and if he
is untaxed will earn £50 per week. If we decide to tax away half
of his income then we will probably not have £25 to redistribute
because the individual may choose to work less hours given that
the reward per hour is much smaller now.

To make this income tax more explicit let us take an example
of two individuals who can earn income, both of whom have
similar utility functions and obtain pleasure from income and
from leisure (see Appendix B). One individual (I) earns twice as
much as the other (II) and we adjust the multiplicative constants
on the utility functions so that both individuals work the same
number of hours when untaxed. Figure 1 shows the utility of
the two individuals as the tax which I pays II is moved from 0%
to 100%.

The aim of the tax if we adopt the utilitarian philosophy is to
maximise the sum of utility of the two individuals and hence we
stop taxing I when the utility he loses from an increase in tax is
equal to the utility gained by II, i.e. when the tax rate is approximately 9.5%. If we adopt the maximin philosophy then we tax

until the utility of II is at the highest level, at approximately 58.5%. If we tax above this level, although II is obtaining a larger percentage of I's income, he cuts down the number of hours he works so much that there is less to redistribute.

A general model of optimal income tax under the maximin concept of justice has been tackled by Professor Atkinson[8] and he compares his results with those of Professor Mirrlees[9] who initially tackled the problem for the utilitarian case. These models have a continuous range of different earning abilities, allow the tax schedules to be non-linear and cover different possible supply of labour functions. While it would take too long to explain the techniques used and conclusions drawn, the tax rates for one example (distribution of earning log-normal) are given below.

	Maximin:		Utilitarian:	
	average	marginal	average	marginal
Median	10	52	6	21
Top decile	28	34	14	21
Top percentile	28	26	15	18
% not working	17%		0%	

The difference between the utilitarian and maximin case in this example is fairly typical, i.e. the maximin tax rates are considerably higher than the utilitarian rates for the better off individuals in society. Also typical of these examples is that while only a minute percentage of the workforce decide not to work in the utilitarian case, about 17% decide not to work in the maximin case. If we choose to redistribute taxes to the worst off individuals in society then we must not be surprised if they decide it is not worth their while working at their lowly paid jobs.

While the comparisons between the utilitarian tax rates and the maximin tax rates are unsurprising the comparisons with the actual tax rates in the UK today are not what we would expect. Obviously the optimal tax rates change as the parameters of the model are changed, but those given here are some of the highest taxes found in the various examples and yet these are still much lower than we experience in the UK today. In the maximin example given, the average tax rate for an individual just in the top one-thousandth of all earners is only 27%. Does this mean that we are taxing income so highly in the UK today that a reduction in income taxes would benefit all members of society,

even the very poorest? This is a view expressed by Sir Keith
Joseph who has recently argued just this point. However, attempts
to discover the disincentive effects of taxes in the UK suggest the
low taxes found in the theoretical examples are so because the
supply of labour functions used are more sensitive to tax changes
than is really the case in real life. Surveys by Break[10] in 1956 and
Fields and Stanbury[11] in 1971, concerning self-employed lawyers
and accountants in the UK, do not suggest the UK tax rates are
great disincentives to work. Break found that 13% of his sample
thought that taxes were a disincentive while 10% thought they
were an incentive to work harder. Fields and Stanbury found that
19% of their sample thought that taxes were a disincentive while
11% found they were encouraged to work harder.

My personal belief is that if we decide to maximise the welfare
of the worst off individuals in the UK today, presumably those
relying on supplementary benefits, then we could increase our
present tax rates and obtain more money to redistribute to the
poor. Our ability to raise money to redistribute to the poor would
probably be curtailed not by the reduction in hours worked but
by the loss of skilled workers to other countries where the tax
rates would be less high. Thus, the optimal tax rates would be
higher if all advanced western countries adopted a maximin concept of justice than if the UK decided to adopt the policy alone.

Education

Economists are interested in education since it can, to
some extent, determine an individual's future earning ability.
Hence, attacking the inequality problem at this stage may
reduce the need to attack the problem through income taxes
later. In order to analyse our specific interest I have assumed
time spent teaching a child is the only way education
determines future earned income; and we look to how different concepts of justice produce different optimal class sizes.
I assume all teachers are of identical ability and, given each
teacher works for the same number of hours, different class
sizes mean different effective teaching time, which I define
as a fixed amount of teaching time divided by the number of
pupils in the class. We assume pupils convert effective teaching time (t) into future income (y) in the form

$$y = af(t)$$

where a differs between pupils of different ability. We assume that each pupil has the same utility function and combining this utility function with the production function (see Appendix C) we obtain a function relating each pupil's utility to the effective teaching time allocated to him:

$$u(t) = n_j v(t)$$

for a pupil of type j where we constrain $v(t)$ to be a strictly concave function.

I have postulated ten ability groups, numbered 1 to 10, type 1 being the least able and type 10 the most able. The class size for pupils of type j, ξj, is given as a percentage of the size of a class of least able children. Obviously, the smaller the class the better off the pupil will be, since smaller classes mean more effective teaching time. We assume for the following examples,

$$v(t) = \frac{1}{1-b} t^{1-b}$$

and produce optimal class sizes for $b = \frac{1}{4}$, $b = \frac{1}{2}$ and $b = \frac{3}{4}$ (see table 1).

Table 1

b		ξ_1	ξ_2	ξ_3	ξ_4	ξ_5	ξ_6	ξ_7	ξ_8	ξ_9	ξ_{10}
$\frac{1}{4}$	U_t	100%	98%	96%	94%	92%	90%	89%	88%	86%	85%
	M_m	100%	114%	128%	142%	157%	172%	187%	203%	219%	235%
$\frac{1}{2}$	U_t	100%	95%	91%	88%	85%	82%	79%	77%	75%	73%
	M_m	100%	121%	144%	169%	196%	225%	256%	289%	324%	361%
$\frac{3}{4}$	U_t	100%	93%	87%	82%	78%	74%	70%	67%	64%	62%
	M_m	100%	146%	201%	286%	384%	506%	655%	835%	1,056%	1,300%

The most immediate thing to notice is that in the maximin case the more able pupils are, the larger is the class, whereas the situation is reversed for the utilitarian case. The present comprehensive system purports to treat all children equally except remedial classes who at present get a larger teacher allocation. Thus, theoretically, the present system is closer to the maximin optimum than the utilitarian one. The pre-comprehensive system would appear to have been closer to the utilitarian system since, ignoring the small number of educationally subnormal children, the distribution of resources tended to favour the better children, e.g. the grammar school pupil, as against the less able pupil.

However, the difference in class sizes required for the maximin case are very large and, to the extent that the model approximates reality, may prove a radical change with the present system, particularly if $v(t)$ takes a form with b close to ¾, which would be the case if the production function $y=af(k)$ exhibited strong decreasing returns to scale. Also, the distribution of abilities assumed here is not large since, if we took a pupil of the lowest ability and one of the highest ability and gave them both the same effective teaching time, the more able pupil would always have less than twice the utility of the least able child. Since in the real world the distribution of abilities may well be less equal than this the different class sizes generated here may be understatements of a real-world case.

Economic Growth

Maximin has been most criticised as a concept of justice because it does not appear to allow scope for any economic growth. The argument for this view is that any poor generation should only save enough to make future generations as well off and no better off. If they saved enough to make future generations better off then they, the least well off, would be reducing their own utility to make better-off generations even richer, which is counter to the maximin concept of justice. The theoretical justification for this comes from models which assume that only one generation, all members of whom are identical, is alive at any one period of time. Now nobody would accept this as being representative of the real world but it has been useful in economic theory as a simplification to study the essential features of a utilitarian optimal growth model, where further refinements only confuse the results. However, since this simplification does not work for the maximin case we should not reject maximin as a concept of justice but realise that the simple model cannot tell us all we need to know in this case and, in consequence, introduce more real-world information.

As a simple example where maximin creates growth, consider the following (see Appendix D). Let us suppose that each generation consists of two types of individuals, one group who produce and save and another who only subsist. Also let us suppose that these individuals care about the capital stock they leave to the next generation. If we left the individuals to their own devices then the unproductive individuals would subsist while the others would consume above this level and also save some capital for the next generation. They may well save enough to make the next generation better off than the first. If we now tax the producers to give to the unproductive and aim to maximise the welfare of the worst off group then the rate of growth will increase since the individuals both enjoy one unit of capital stock left to the next generation while they must always share today's consumption. It is almost certainly not a feature of most maximin growth models that the rate of growth will be higher than in the laissez-faire situation. However, what is a feature of this model, and is almost certainly a general feature, is that the optimal growth rate using the utilitarian philosophy will be higher than the optimal growth rate using the maximin philosophy. The reason is that when we determine the rate of saving in the maximin case we maximise the utility of the unproductive members of the first generation, which depends only on their own consumption and the capital stock they leave. In the utilitarian case the consumption of all future generations enters our calculations and these will be higher the higher the saving of the first generation. Thus, the counteracting benefit of the loss of consumption of the first generation is much larger in the utilitarian case than the maximin case. The fact that the maximin growth path may require a slower rate of growth than the utilitarian growth path will be considered by many to be an advantage were we to adopt the concept of justice in the UK at present. However, it may be less attractive to underdeveloped countries who view economic growth, even at the expense of the present generation, as a major target.

Conclusion

It is worth pointing out here that Rawls believes his theory of justice to be all-embracing, principles which are relevant for all societies at all periods of time. However, this view has been criticised, basically because Rawls believes that income, wealth and power are primary goods, goods desired by all individuals in all societies. However, there have been societies and exist societies, e.g. China, where the possession of wealth and earning of incomes higher than your neighbour is considered to be harmful to the

character. Thus Rawls's concept of justice is generally considered
to be applicable only to a modern western society. Hence, I feel
it is meaningful to attempt to use economic theory to predict
how the adoption of the principle in the UK would affect our
economic system on the understanding it would not be adopted
elsewhere.

To the extent that the above models represent the system, the
most surprising conclusion I find is that the changes required
would probably not be as radical as one would at first expect.
Certainly the changes in income tax and education, while they
would reduce our present national product, are not out of sympathy with the views of many individuals who feel we should
redistribute to the poor. However, individuals who worry about
the lowly paid in society tend to advocate growth as a means of
improving their absolute level of welfare. This view is frequently
held because of the belief that the present distribution of income
will not change radically over the years. If the slowdown in
growth is accompanied by the move to a maximin reallocation of
goods in each period of time, then the growth implications of
maximin may be more acceptable and this apparent contradiction
may be lost.

I wish now to turn briefly to the problem of the relevance of
principles of justice chosen from the hypothetical position of
being uncertain of one's place in society. Given that in any real
world voting system individuals do know their place in society,
do such concepts of justice have any practical significance?
Clearly, the distribution of abilities, and sensitivity of labour
supply to tax rates, will rarely if ever take the form that the maximin principle will be voted for by individuals voting to maximise
their own consumption. However, one can argue that individuals
do not vote purely to maximise their own consumption. Given
the average age of a voter, the probability of their having a prolonged illness which would require enormous medical fees to cure
can be estimated quite accurately, and the bad risk individuals,
who would be unable to buy private health insurance, will be
easily identifiable. And yet there is no great opposition to the
state national health service where bad risk individuals pay no
more than a healthy individual who never enters hospital. This is
an example of the way individuals are willing to put themselves
in other people's shoes and are happy to provide free medical aid
to someone who will never repay the debt to society. Thus, when
a society chooses its concept of justice, through its choice of

economic instruments, it is probable that individuals are not choosing principles which maximise their expected consumption. Thus we are not talking of concepts of justice that will never be adopted in a democratic society. The possibility that at some point in the future a maximin concept of justice would be chosen by society is very real.

Appendix A

In order for an individual's choices over uncertain prospects to be represented by a utility function, the individual must satisfy four axioms, the strongest of which is the following. If an individual is indifferent between two alternatives Q_1 and Q_2 ($Q_1 \sim Q_2$) then the following must always hold:

$$p_1 Q_1 + p_2 Q_3 \sim p_1 Q_2 + p_2 Q_3.$$

For Harsanyi's analyses to hold, individuals must all satisfy these four axioms.

Consider the following problem where we have two bundles X_1 and X_2, two individuals A and B, and A and B must choose the size of X_1 and X_2. It is uncertain which individual will get which bundle (px_1 is probability A gets X_1 and px_2 is the probability A gets X_2). Suppose there exist two alternatives α and β. We confront a third individual with a choice between α and β, call this choice ψ_2. Below we show the probability for A (B's follows automatically).

$$\psi_2$$

α	$px_1 = \frac{2}{3}$	$px_2 = \frac{1}{3}$
β	$px_1 = \frac{1}{3}$	$px_2 = \frac{2}{3}$

If we add the assumption that A and B are identical then the third individual may well be indifferent between α and β ($\alpha \sim \beta$).

Suppose now we widen our choices by adding another state ψ_1, with one alternative γ:

$$\psi_1 \qquad\qquad \psi_2$$

$\gamma \quad px_1 = \frac{2}{3} px_2 = \frac{1}{3}$ $\qquad \alpha \quad px_1 = \frac{2}{3} px_2 = \frac{1}{3}$

$\qquad\qquad\qquad\qquad\qquad \beta \quad px_1 = \frac{1}{3} px_2 = \frac{2}{3}.$

If ψ_1 and ψ_2 have an equal chance of occurring and they are mutually exclusive then compounding these

$$1/2\gamma + 1/2\alpha \qquad px_1 = \tfrac{2}{3}px_2 = \tfrac{1}{3}$$
$$1/2\gamma + 1/2\beta \qquad px_1 = \tfrac{1}{2}px_2 = \tfrac{1}{2}.$$

If the third individual favours the Rawlsian view of the type of uncertainty A and B should face when choosing X_1 and X_2 he will be indifferent between the two alternatives as long as the individuals do not know the probabilities.

However, if the individual believes the Harsanyi type of uncertainty he will prefer alternative two to alternative one, since each individual has an equal chance of obtaining each commodity bundle. But we now have,

$$\alpha \sim \beta$$
$$1/2\gamma + 1/2\beta > 1/2\gamma + 1/2\alpha$$

which does not satisfy the above axiom.

Appendix B

We assume the utilities take the following form,

I $2(wl)^{1/2} + 2(1-l)^{1/2}$

II $2(wl)^{1/2} + 2\delta(1-l)^{1/2}$

and determine δ so that if there exists no tax then both individuals work the same amount of time. Setting $w_I = 1$ and taxing I to redistribute to II we derive the following indirect utility functions:

$$\text{I} \qquad 2\left(\frac{t^2 - 2t + 1}{2 - k}\right)^{1/2} + 2\left(\frac{1}{2 - t}\right)^{1/2}$$

$$\text{II} \qquad 2\left(\frac{w}{2} + \frac{3t - 3t^2}{4 - 2t}\right)^{1/2} + 2\delta\left(\frac{1}{2} - \frac{t - t^2}{4w - 2wt}\right)^{1/2}$$

Setting $w_{II} = 0.5$ the results shown in the text are easily derived. To determine the optimal maximin tax rate we note the tax take from I is $(t - t^2)/(2 - t)$. This is maximised at the point $t^2 - 4t + 2 = 0$ which has a unique solution in the unit interval.

Appendix C

Taking the production and the utility function we have,

$$U[af(t)]$$

and if $U(-)$ is homogeneous then this can be rewritten[12]:

$$\psi(a)\, U[f(t)] \quad \text{or} \quad n_j v(t).$$

We assume $v(k)$ is a strictly concave function and doubly differentiable throughout. A necessary condition for a utilitarian optimum is $n_j v'(t_j) = n_1 v'(t_1)$ and normalising we find $n_j v'(w/\xi_j) = v'(w/\xi_1)$ where w is the teacher's total time available. Given the form of the utility function $n_j = v'(\xi_j/\xi_1)$ thus $\xi_j = \xi_1 v'^{-1}(n_j)$. A necessary condition for a maximin optimum in this case is $n_j v(k) = n_1 v(k)$. Normalising and solving gives $\xi_j = \xi_1 v'(n_j/c)$, where c is $(1-b)$ for this utility function. We assume $n_2 = 1.1$, $n_3 = 1.2$, etc and redefine the ξ_j's as percentages of ξ_1 to give the table in the text.

Appendix D

We assume the capital stock at each generation is k, of which $k-s$ is consumed and s is saved, producing as capital for the next generation. Each individual's utility function takes the form,

$$U(k_0 - s_0) + \delta U(as_0)$$

and I use the function $U(x) = (1/1-b)x^{1-b}$ and define subsistence as $U(0) = 0$. If we look at the competitive case we only need look to the individuals who produce who maximise $U(k_0 - s_0) + \delta U(as_0)$ giving:

$$s_0 = (1 + a^{(b-1)/b}\, \delta^{-1/b})^{-1}k_0,$$

If we now make the producers pay tax to the non-producers and assume the supply of labour is fixed, the maximum saving rate is,

$$s_0 = [1 + 2a(2a\delta)^{-1/b}]^{-1}k_0$$

which will be larger than the competitive case if $0 < b < 1$.

In the utilitarian case we assume all generations will save at the same rate, thus we have an infinite objective function the solution to which is:

$$\frac{(as_0)^b}{(\frac{1}{2}k_0 - \frac{1}{2}s_0)^b} - 2a\delta = \frac{(as_0)^b a(1 - k_0^{-1} 2s_0)}{[as_0(1 - k_0^{-1} s_0)]^b} + (as_0)^b T \qquad (1)$$

where

$$T = \sum_{t=2}^{\infty} \frac{k_0^{-1} at[ts_0^{t-1} - (t+1)s_0^t]}{[k_0^{-1} a^t s_0^t (1 - s_0)]^b} + \sum_{t=2}^{\infty} \frac{k_0^{-1} a^{t+1}(t+1)s_0^t}{[k_0^{-1} a^{t+1} s_0^{t+1}]^b}$$

Calling the left-hand side of eqn. (1) $Z(s_0)$, the maximin solution required $Z(s_0) = 0$ whereas since the right-hand side of (1) is positive for all s_0 the utilitarian solution requires $Z(s_0) > 0$. It can be seen,

$$Z'(s_0) = \left[(2s_0)^2 \left(\frac{k_0}{2s_0} - \frac{1}{2} \right)^{2+b} \right]^{-1} 2a^{1+b} k_0 > 0.$$

Hence the utilitarian saving rate is higher than the maximum saving rate.

Notes and References

1 J. Rawls, *A Theory of Justice*, Oxford University Press 1972.
2 G. Debreu, *A Theory of Value*, John Wiley 1959.
3 K. J. Arrow, An extension of the basic theorem of classical welfare economics, *Proceedings of the Second Berkeley Symposium on Mathematical Statistics and Probability*.
4 J. de V. Graaff, *Theoretical Welfare Economics*, Cambridge University Press. 1957.
5 W. Baumol, *Welfare Economics and the Theory of the State*, Longmans 1952.
6 K. Arrow, *Social Choice and Individual Values*, John Wiley 1951.
7 Harsanyi, 'Cardinal welfare, individualist ethics and interpersonal comparisons of utility', *Journal of Political Economy* 1955.
8 A. Atkinson, *Maximin and Optimal Income Tax*, Essex Discussion Paper No. 47.
9 J. A. Mirrlees, 'An exploration in the theory of optimal income taxation', *Review of Economic Studies* 1971.
10 Break, 'Income taxes and incentives to work', *American Economic Review* 1957.
11 Fields and Stanbury, 'Income tax and incentives to work', *American Economic Review* 1971.
12 A. Katz, 'Comments on the definition of homogeneous and homothetic functions', *Journal of Economic Theory* 1971.

TIM TUTTON
The City University

10 Intellectual conceptions of economic justice *

This paper is not a description of what economists have said about economic justice. It is about some of the ways in which the development of economics as an academic discipline has tended to influence the way in which 'economists' look at ethical issues in economics.

To survey the argument briefly: the origins of 'economic science' were inextricably bound up with the desire by individuals to influence government economic policy. A necessary condition for this influence was the attainment of scientific respectability. The interaction between the desire to influence economic policy and the consequent need to be considered 'scientific' has tended to produce a particular way of looking at normative issues in economics.

The interaction has been such that economics has not simply provided the political structure with a 'menu' of economic policies from which the structure chooses those which are consistent with its own value judgements. Instead, economists have tended to preselect those value judgements which can be 'acceptably' combined with the analysis to give policy recommendations. This process of preselection has tended to confer the apparent approval of 'scientific economics' on particular policy objectives in a way which would seem to flout deeply held convictions about the

* The author would like to thank Professor Bernard Corry for comments on a preliminary draft of this paper.

149

impossibility of deducing 'ought' statements from 'is' statements.

The conclusion will not simply be that some economists are politically conservative — and have an understandable tendency to smuggle value judgements into apparently positive theorising when trying to write persuasively. It will be, rather, that the sort of pressures which have created economics as an academic discipline — the twin drives towards policy influence and scientific respectability — have themselves tended to create a particular bias in looking at ethical issues in economics, have effectively tended to create a particular theory of economic justice.

From the alleged beginnings of 'economic science' its practitioners have faced a credibility gap when it has come to saying what 'ought to be' in the economic sphere. Back in the 17th century — as recounted by Letwin in his book *The Origins of Scientific Economics*[1] — a major problem for writers on economic affairs was that they themselves had, and were known to have, strong financial interests in the outcome of their policy recommendations. Men like Sir Josiah Child were merchants. Their main policy recommendations — lower interest rates for example — tended to involve a better deal for merchants. They may have had the best 'scientific' and highest 'ethical' reasons for such recommendations but it was not surprising that their ideas were treated with some scepticism. To quote Letwin:

> Apart from being thought original, Child wanted also to be considered objective . . . But a reputation for objectivity was very difficult to achieve in the seventeenth century; being designated an expert did not automatically assure anyone that the expert's proposals were disinterested. On the contrary, men evidently believed that anyone's recommendations on economic affairs ought to be examined suspiciously because they might always be directed rather by the writer's private interests than by a disinterested concern for the public good.[2]

As Letwin points out, the only people who might have been listened to with any respect — on account of their learning and 'otherworldliness' — were the scholars in the universities. But they did not consider commerce a proper area for academic study.[3]

To overcome the suspicion of special pleading two strategies tended to be favoured by those intent on influencing government policy. On the one hand, there was the time honoured tradition in pamphleteering of anonymity. This, however, could only be expected to be successful to a very limited extent. It might be that the author avoided identification as the author of a particular pamphlet but this in itself was unlikely to eliminate the suspicion that the author had dark motives for his proposals. What was needed was to be able to appeal for support to some higher authority than the individual's own opinions. A standard option in the past had been the invoking of the authority of religion. But, even though Calvinism might identify profitability with godliness, it did not do anything to show that higher merchant profits would provide more worldly benefits to society as a whole.

Increasingly amongst economic writers the higher authority which they sought was the authority of 'science'. If it could be seen to be proved 'scientifically' that, say, lower interest rates were 'in the public interest', then the force of the argument was going to be little affected by the knowledge that the author of the proof was going to gain from such a policy. The increasing emphasis on deductive reasoning and 'scientific method' during the 17th century by people like Sir Dudley North culminated in Adam Smith. But, as Letwin says, the 17th century economists 'created scientific theories, yet they generally did not do so deliberately, nor did they do it for the sake of knowledge, but rather their scientific accomplishments were a by-product of their efforts to convince others to accede to certain economic policies.'[4]

The problem has been, though, that 'science' has not remained simply a passive tool for persuasion. On the one hand, economists needed science as support for their proposals. On the other hand, science itself makes demands. For so-called 'positive' economics the scientization of the subject has brought with it tendencies which have come up for recurrent methodological criticism. The desire by economists to be considered scientists — on a par with natural scientists — has meant a selection of areas for study on the basis of their amenability to 'scientific' method. Preferably this has meant amenability to mathematical method.

The desire to say only things which were 'scientific' has, however, had even more fundamental implications in the field of 'normative' economics. In normative economics it is not just that certain areas are more quantifiable or other areas less expressible in terms of set theory. The problem of being 'scientific' has, rather, been the logical impossibility of deducing 'ought' statements from 'is' statements. 'Ought' statements require values, opinions, subjectivity — hardly the sort of objective sanctification that the 17th century economists wanted for their policy proposals.

One response to this situation has been to say that economics as a science — and economists as scientists — have nothing to say on normative issues. They can say nothing about whether one situation is more just than another, nothing about whether one policy is more just than another. This solution has not been generally acceptable to economists. It was never likely to be. The point of science for the 17th century economists and for many of their successors was to influence policy. Scientific respectability was a necessary means to this influence — it was not an end in itself.

The standard way out of the problem has been to start by admitting that it is logically impossible to deduce normative statements from positive statements. The next stage is then to say that it is nevertheless possible to select value premises which are themselves 'noncontroversial'. If there is no disagreement about the only values used in deriving policy conclusions, then, so the argument goes, nothing has happened to contravene the objective status of these conclusions. Crucially, 'more or less noncontroversial' is translated into 'more or less scientific'. The problem, then, is to find noncontroversial value judgements which will be of any use in deriving policy conclusions.

At first glance, a theoretical answer to the problem of finding values on which the community in some sense agrees would seem to lie in the use of social welfare functions. The social welfare function is seen as in some sense providing the community's 'preferences', which are combined with the economist's 'analysis' to produce policy conclusions. At second glance, however, social welfare functions seem to raise more problems than they solve. There has, for instance, been the long and abstruse debate on whether and under what conditions social welfare functions have even a theoretical existence, let alone a practical value. At third glance, one can see why social welfare functions would not be a very attractive idea to many policy minded economists even if all the theoretical and practical problems with them could be solved.

The argument has been so far that the twin motivations behind much of the development in economics have been, on the one hand, the desire of economists to be considered scientists and, on the other hand, their desire to influence economic policy. Even social welfare functions which 'worked' would not score very high in assisting the simultaneous achievement of these two objectives. On the one hand, if the economist himself specifies the 'weights' given to individual preferences in deriving the social welfare function, then there is nothing very objective or scientific about that. On the other hand, if those weights are going to be provided by the community — by opinion polls or some other means — then the role of the economist is explicitly reduced to that of a technician. The community says what it wants; the economist provides the most 'efficient' way of satisfying those wants. This is not a role to satisfy either the 17th century economists or a large number of their 20th century counterparts.

What the successor to Child and North wants is quite simply to say what government economic policy ought to be. He therefore wants to be able to specify the necessary values himself while not relinquishing his claim to objectivity. To achieve both these aims he has — on the theory propounded above — to select value judgements which are generally seen as being 'noncontroversial'. The question then is: what is 'noncontroversiality' likely to entail? What will characterise value judgements which are going to be accepted as noncontroversial?

In economic policy the most critical value judgements tend to relate to the 'distribution' of the costs and benefits of particular policies. Most value judgements about distribution tend to be extremely controversial; especially because the distributional value judgements in which policy makers are likely to be interested are not concerned so much with distribution as such as they are with 'redistribution'. Any policy which involves taking resources away from one group of people and giving them to another group of people is likely to be a subject of conflict and controversy between the two groups. The question then becomes: what will characterise noncontroversial value judgements relating to the redistribution of resources between groups of people?

One answer is that a main characteristic of noncontroversial value judgements in this area will be that they cater for the lowest common denominator in altruism or enlightened self-interest existing in the community. Any redistribution sanctioned by everyone in the community will represent the most that *all* those who 'have' are prepared to concede to those who do not 'have'. In other words, the values invoked are not really 'consensus' values in any global sense of the term. Instead, they represent a consensus of the values of those from whom redistribution will 'take'. Seen in this way noncontroversiality might seem a fairly dubious, and certainly a very subjective, ally.

But often it is not seen in this way. Instead, noncontroversiality is seen as evidence of objectivity. Thus A. J. Culyer, in his now standard textbook on the economics of social policy,[5] grandly admits that one cannot get entirely rid of normative considerations from problems of policy prescription but goes on to claim that the use of noncontroversial or 'weak' value judgements makes such judgements 'a good deal less subjective than otherwise they might be.'

The logical extreme in such noncontroversial value judgements is the Paretian one, that a situation can only be said to have improved when at least one person gains and when no one person loses. Now there is nothing novel about accusations of implicit conservatism levelled at Paretian economics. The point here is that Paretian economics is just a special case of the theory of economic justice which is a logical outcome of the context in which economics has developed. Unlike the development of some other academic disciplines, the intellectualisation process in economics has to a great extent been a means to political ends — a means to influencing government economic policy. The means to this end has been the attainment of intellectual and scientific respectability. Influencing policy while remaining 'scientific' has entailed in some sense 'neutralising' the subjective, 'anti-scientific', aspects of essentially political value judgements. This neutralisation has been achieved by translating the phrase 'non-controversial value judgement' into the phrase 'quasi-scientific proposition'.

This tendency of 'scientific economics' to try to imply a theory of economic justice reached its apparent apotheosis with the so-called 'new welfare economics'. The problem with the simple Paretian value judgement as defined above was its restriction to situations where no redistribution took place. Although it might be satisfying to simple conservatives to exclude from 'scientific' discussion (and therefore from discussion generally) those situations which involve redistribution, it hardly suited those who wanted to be 'scientific' about economic policy to have a whole potential area of economic theorising ruled out of bounds.

The result of this conflict, between academic imperialism and a logic which said that the normative needed values, was the literature of hypothetical compensation criteria mainly associated with the names of Kaldor, Hicks and Scitovsky.[6] The driving force behind these writings was the attempt to classify certain distributions of resources as preferable to others without invoking ethical judgements about whether one distribution or another was more desirable *per se*.

The attempt has been repeatedly judged a failure by the 'giants' of neo-classical welfare economics — Little, Samuelson, Graaff among others.[7] But despite this, the endeavour to be 'objective' when evaluating distributions of resources, a hallmark of Paretian welfare economics, survives. It survives in Culyer's labelling of the Paretian value judgement as less subjective than other value judgements. It survives, perhaps most crudely of all, in an essay by Harberger quoted with a mixture of awe and horror in a recently published book by Rowley and Peacock.[8] In this essay Harberger 'solves' the conflict between values and objectivity by stipulating simply that 'when evaluating the net benefits or costs of a given action (project, programme, or policy) the costs and benefits accruing to each member of the relevant group (e.g. a nation) should normally be added without regard to the individual(s) to whom they accrue.'[9]

The Paretian philosophy survives, perhaps most subtly, in the changing attitudes over the last few years within British economics towards full employment as a prime objective of government economic policy. There can be little doubt about the relevance of a high level of employment to the achievement of economic justice. Even those with the most conservative beliefs recognise a need to help those who are worst off. It is now a hallmark of conservative philosophy that social policy should be aimed at those who 'really need' help. High unemployment hits those who are worst off both directly and indirectly. It hits them directly because it is among the groups which have least that unemployment tends to be highest. Whether 'disadvantaged' groups are classified by colour, by region, by education levels, it is those who are worst off to start with whose unemployment levels tend to rise fastest when aggregate unemployment rises.

Some of the indirect effects of unemployment are equally relevant to economic justice. Even those who frown on direct cash handouts to low income groups tend to talk about at least 'helping the poor to help themselves', giving them opportunities to improve their position in society, and so on. A central effect of high unemployment will tend to be a reduction of opportunities for upward social mobility.[10] When labour markets are tight, employers are encouraged to relax their hiring standards, to take on people without the levels of human capital investment which might hitherto have been required. Employers are encouraged to rethink racial aspects of hiring and promotion policies. Tight labour markets increase the costs of ignoring particular sources of labour supply. In other words, full employment is a very important issue when discussing economic justice.

For a large part of the post war period full employment was a consensus objective of economic policy amongst both British politicians and economic academia. It was not the sole objective. The consensus did not doubt that there were times when the objectives of full employment would conflict with, and be sacrificed to, the achievement of other objectives, e.g. balance of payments equilibrium. But even though there might be balance-of-payments-correcting hiccups along the way, these were seen as essentially short-term deviations from the attainment of full employment as the primary goal of economic management.

The conventional framework of economic policy sees governments as being mainly preoccupied with five objectives relating to employment, the balance of payments, the rate of economic growth, the rate of inflation, and the distribution of income. But not all these have been seen in the past as of equal importance. For much of the post war period the UK government tended to emphasise the maximisation of the level of employment subject to the constraint of the balance of payments.[11] The Conservatives might in principle place a rather higher weighting on the external objective but a combination of Butskellite philosophy and electoral pragmatism tended to prevent this from getting out of hand. Inflation might rear its head but for the most part this tended to be seen as a matter for various sorts of incomes policy rather than as a constraint on demand management.

However, in 1975, this consensus on the long-term importance of the full employment objective no longer seems to exist. Scattered throughout the 'serious' press are articles by academic economists talking about the need for the UK to accept as normal levels of unemployment which would have been unthinkable in the relatively recent past. One such piece quoted the opinion of an eminent British economist that the so-called 'natural' level of unemployment for the UK was now of the order of 3¾% of the labour force.[12]

A recent book on economic policy from the mainstream of British academic economics — Professor Meade's *The Intelligent Radical's Guide to Economic Policy*[13] — does not even list the level of employment as one of the 'intelligent radical's' objectives of economic policy. Meade does see the level of employment as a constraint when selecting an appropriate anti-inflation policy, but there is nothing about *full* employment in the chapter entitled 'The objectives of economic policy'.

So what has caused this reaction against full employment? For some economists the change has simply been a change in the 'situation' facing the UK economy. Their feelings about unemployment are a reaction to the scale of current inflation and balance of payments problems. For these people there has not necessarily been any change in their feelings about the long-run primacy of full employment as an objective of economic policy. But for other economists something less than full employment is now seen as a permanent target of economic policy. Behind this thinking lies the emergence (or, arguably, the re-emergence) of two theoretical orthodoxies.

On the one hand is the 'monetarist' view of the relation between the level of unemployment and the rate of inflation. On this view there is no long-run trade-off between unemployed and inflation. The lowest level of unemployment which can be achieved without a continually accelerating rate of inflation is the so-called 'natural' rate of unemployment. So what is the current natural rate of unemployment for the UK? Formal definitions of this rather metaphysical concept tend to be equally metaphysical, talking in terms of the rate of unemployment which is thrown up when the economic system is in 'full Walrasian general equilibrium'. Slightly less mystically, the natural rate of unemployment tends to be identified with the sum of 'frictional' and 'structural' unemployment in the economy. And this is where the second theoretical orthodoxy enters.

This says that, since around the end of 1966, the 'structure' of unemployment in the UK has gone through significant changes. In particular, it is argued, increases in unemployment and other social security benefits have increased the volume of 'search' or 'voluntary' or 'frictional' unemployment; and have therefore raised the level of the natural rate of unemployment as well as, conveniently, reducing the hardship costs of a given volume of unemployment. If one then speculates about other 'structural' changes the UK economy might be going through as the combined result of entry into the Common Market, the rise in oil prices, the development of North Sea oil, the alleged need for industries crippled by decades of inefficiency and underinvestment to go to the wall, etc., then one soon arrives at estimates of the natural rate of unemployment like the one of 3¾% quoted above. One takes such estimates and such theorising as seriously as one feels inclined, perhaps remembering in passing that the last period in the UK's history of chronic deficient demand and unemployment — in the 1930s — brought forth a similar chorus of mutterings about the 'structural' reasons for the unemployment levels of the day.

From the angle of this paper the point of all this is that, although these theories are related to the fall from grace of the full employment objective, they do not by themselves adequately explain it. After all, monetarism has not yet conquered British economics. 'Monetarists', or at least 'strong' monetarists believing in the zero unemployment/inflation trade-off, are probably still a minority in the academic economic establishment. Similarly, although there may be a fair degree of agreement that there have been changes in the structure of unemployment in the UK since 1966, no such agreement exists on the quantitative extent of these changes.[14] In particular, there is little agreement on just how much extra unemployment has resulted from changes on the labour supply side. What has happened — partly because of monetarist and monetarist-related theorising — is that the paramount importance of full employment has ceased to be a non-controversial value judgement.

In the period of post-Keynesian-revolution euphoria a main attraction of the Keynesian message was that, balance of payments apart, increasing the level of employment by increasing the level of effective demand seemed such a costless exercise. Those who were out of work got jobs. No one else seemed to lose anything very much. Real classic Paretian stuff. The costlessness of increasing employment was formalised in the practice of imputing zero shadow prices to unemployed and under-employed labour in the development plans of developing countries. As the fifties and sixties wore on, economists became more interested in the inflationary implications of low levels of unemployment. The Phillips curve had its heyday. But even such a pronounced conservative as Professor Paish was still talking in 1968 in terms of a target rate of unemployment of 2¼%.[15]

At the time Paish was writing, the trade-off between unemployment and inflation was still seen as favourable enough to make relatively low unemployment levels relatively costless. Additionally, there was the view that a moderate rate of price inflation was good for business because it seemed to enable firms to keep prices ahead of wages and therefore was a help to profits. In 1975 the monetarist-influenced view is that the costs of keeping unemployment at the levels of earlier periods are now substantial.

It might still be that combining a social welfare function which did not give particularly radical weights to the interests of low income groups with some plausible thinking on the longer run relation between unemployment and inflation — perhaps in the context of some form of incomes policy — would imply target levels of unemployment which could be recognised as close relations of yesteryear's full employment. This would be the outcome of recognising that there might be significant costs in holding unemployment below a certain level but of them going on to argue that the benefits of such a policy would outweigh the costs. But such an argument would not receive the blessing of the theory of economic justice which only sanctions the use of value judgements which are 'not really subjective'.

The conclusion must be that the spirit of the new welfare economics — the desire to evaluate economic policies without the apparent aid of value judgements — lives on despite repeated methodological annihilation. Rowley and Peacock marvel at 'the remarkable survivorship capacity of this hardy dogma'[16] (i.e. Paretian welfare economics) but they offer little to explain its resilience. Marxists see neoclassical economics as just part of the ideological superstructure of capitalism — as an apologetic for the interests of the bourgeoisie. Paretian welfare economics is then simply seen as part of neoclassical economics. But this explanation fits the part less easily than the whole. Within neoclassical economics there would seem to be other, less methodologically suspect, ways of defending the status quo — Rowley and Peacock's 'liberalist' welfare economics for example.

A more obvious explanation of the 'survivorship capacity' of Paretian economics, and of all attempts to minimise and conceal the role of ethics and subjectivity in normative economics, would seem to lie in their function as an apologetic not so much for the interests of the bourgeoisie as a whole as for the interests of economists.

A dominant characteristic of welfare economics in the tradition of Marshall and Pigou was its preoccupation with the 'social question'. As expressed by Winch in his book *Economics and Policy*, Marshall

... had been drawn into the study of economics by an interest in practical ethics. How could the lives of the majority of mankind be improved and ennobled? What were the material limitations to human progress? It was possible for him to claim that his life had been devoted to the study of poverty, 'and that very little of my work has been devoted to an inquiry which does not bear on that.' He was fully aware of the importance of making a distinction between the 'positive' issues which concern economic science and 'normative' matters of economic policy. But he did not feel that economics should be confined to questions which were amenable to scientific treatment.[17]

For economists in the tradition of Marshall and Pigou a logical reaction to the failure of the new welfare economics to deal with redistribution without ethics (even if they bothered to take note of the attempt) would have been confirmation in their belief as to the importance of 'practical ethics' to welfare economics. The Paretian reaction to the demonstrable inseparability of ethics and redistribution has, on the other hand, been confirmation in their lack of interest in redistribution — witness the above quote from Harberger for example. In itself this could simply mean that Paretian economics is about 'pure' science unsullied by policy considerations. But Paretian economics has always been very much about policy. So, if Paretian economics is not about 'doing good' in the Marshallian sense, and if it is not about pure science, what is it about?

Partly, Paretian economics is about conservative politics. The absence of the Pigovian interest in 'improving' the distribution of income in Paretian economics helps to make it a suitable framework for conservative thinking. The strongly Paretian flavour in the literary output of the Institute of Economic Affairs testifies to this suitability.

But secondly, and perhaps more importantly from the point of view of understanding its continuing influence, Paretian economics is about the 'role' of the economist in the formulation of economic policy. In a world where the distinction between positive and normative is clear cut, the role of the economist is very much that of the technician. He may venture ethical opinions. But they are no more than that — his opinions. This demarcation of his role is implicit in the general idea of a social welfare function and its role in the optimisation of social welfare.

Paretian economics tends to muddy the distinction between positive and normative by creating a class of value judgements which are 'not entirely subjective' (*viz.* Culyer). This gives the economist much more scope — in a sense much more 'power'. Paretian economics, with its inbuilt value system, centring especially on its attitude to distribution, seemingly allows economists to deduce policy conclusions without going 'outside the science' to get the necessary values. Policy conclusions seem to flow smoothly from economic science through the medium of economic scientists. At times the 'scenario' envisaged by Paretians seems to be one in which conventional roles are reversed and the politicians appear as 'advisers' on how to market the policies which economists have created. Effectively, Paretianism embodies the dream of Letwin's seventeenth century economists, the dream of 'power through science'. It is not surprising that it is defended so tenaciously.

It may not seem much like progress to go from a world of Marshallian preoccupation with practical ethics to one which admits a concern with poverty only when the consciousness of it creates an 'externality' for the rich. But may be that is what is meant by the notion that economics is too important to be left to the economists.

Notes and References

1 W. Letwin, *The Origins of Scientific Economics*, Methuen 1963.
2 Letwin, p 19.
3 Letwin, p 83.
4 Letwin, p ix.
5 A. J. Culyer, *The Economics of Social Policy*, Martin Robertson 1973, p 6.
6 See, for example, N. Kaldor, 'Welfare comparisons of economics and interpersonal comparisons of utility', *Economic Journal*, September 1939.

   J. R. Hicks, 'The foundations of welfare economics', *Economic Journal*, December 1939.

   T. Scitovsky, 'A note on welfare propositions in economics', *Review of Economic Studies*, November 1941; Reprinted in *Readings in Welfare Economics*, K. J. Arrow and T. Scitovsky (eds.), Allen and Unwin 1969.
7 See, for example, I. M. D. Little, *A Critique of Welfare Economics*, 2nd edn., Oxford University Press 1957.

   P. A. Samuelson, 'Evaluation of real national income', *Oxford Economic Papers*, 1950. Reprinted in *Economic Justice*, E. S. Phelps (ed.), Penguin 1973.

   J. de V. Graaff, *Theoretical Welfare Economics*, Cambridge University Press 1957.
8 C. K. Rowley and A. T. Peacock, *Welfare Economics — A Liberal Restatement*, Martin Robertson 1975.
9 A. C. Harberger, 'Three basic postulates for applied welfare economics: an interpretive essay', *Journal of Economic Literature*, September 1971, p 785.
10 See, for example, A. Okun, 'Upward mobility in a high pressure economy', *Brookings Papers on Economic Activity* 1973.
11 See, for example, R. C. O. Matthews, 'Postwar business cycles in the United Kingdom', in *Is The Business Cycle Obsolete?*, M. Bronfenbrenner (ed.)., Wiley 1969.
12 Malcolm Crawford, 'Must one million always be jobless?' *Sunday Times*,

3 August 1975.
13 J. E. Meade, *The Intelligent Radical's Guide to Economic Policy*, Allen & Unwin 1975.
14 See, for example, J. Bowers *et al.*, 'Some aspects of unemployment and the labour market', *National Institute Economic Review*, November 1972.
15 F. W. Paish and J. Hennessy, *Policy for Incomes?*, 4th edn., Institute of Economic Affairs 1968, p 28.
16 Rowley and Peacock, p 3.
17 D. N. Winch, *Economics and Policy*, Hodder and Stoughton 1969, p 31.

Index